THE 12 KEY NOVEL CONSTRUCTION

YOUR BLUEPRINT FOR BUILDING A STRONG STORY

C. S. LAKIN

THE WRITER'S TOOLBOX SERIES

THE 12 KEY PILLARS OF NOVEL CONSTRUCTION by C. S. Lakin

ISBN-10: 0991389476

ISBN-13: 978-0-9913894-7-6

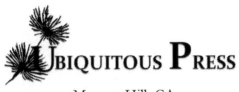

UBIQUITOUS PRESS
Morgan Hill, CA

Books by C. S. Lakin

Writing Craft

Shoot Your Novel: Cinematic Techniques to Supercharge Your Writing

Writing the Heart of Your Story: The Secret to Crafting an Unforgettable Novel

Say What? The Fiction Writer's Handy Guide to Grammar, Punctuation, and Word Usage

Contemporary Suspense/Mystery

Someone to Blame

Conundrum

Innocent Little Crimes

A Thin Film of Lies

Intended for Harm

Fantasy/Sci-Fi

The Wolf of Tebron

The Map across Time

The Land of Darkness

The Unraveling of Wentwater

The Crystal Scepter

The Sands of Ethryn

The Hidden Kingdom

Time Sniffers

Table of Contents

Foreword

Since there are hundreds of writing craft books already published that teach novel structure, why in the world would I write one to add to the pile? Good question, and I'll give you my answer. I wrote this book (which is a compilation, and much more, of a year-long course I did on my blog Live Write Thrive) because I want to help writers get a clear, helpful, and precise understanding of basic novel construction.

I critique and edit more than two hundred partial and complete manuscripts a year. Year after year, I see struggling writers making the same fatal mistakes in their manuscripts. Even those writers who have studied the best novel-writing instruction books, have followed writers' blogs, and have taken numerous workshops *still* don't get the structure.

Why Bother with Structure?

Is structure important? Do I think novelists have to follow very specific structural rules to write a great novel? Yes and yes. When I first started writing novels, I thought I could wing it. I'd read plenty of novels of various genres all my life, so, in a way, I felt that made me an expert. I assumed that by osmosis I'd learned how to write well. And that was true—to a point.

Truth is, a lot of writers believe they can write a novel without taking time to learn the nuts and bolts of novel construction. I wonder why this is. I doubt many aspiring doctors, dentists, or lawyers believe they can jump into their practice by just reading a few books, or maybe even watching some TV shows. I certainly wouldn't want to learn that my surgeon *hadn't* graduated medical school or memorized *Gray's Anatomy* as I was being wheeled on a gurney into the operating arena.

Writing a novel may not be as complex as performing an operation on someone, but it does have its complexities. Just as with building a house—which is what we are going to compare novel writing to in this book—writers have to adeptly wield not only a whole lot of materials but a lot of tools as well. For every task required in building a house, a builder must know both his materials and his tools. You don't frame up a house with tar paper, and you don't use plastic pipe for gas lines. It takes time and effort to acquire the proper training to be proficient in any vocation. Novel writing is no exception.

A Waste of Time

I will venture to say that at least 80-90 percent of the novels I critique are seriously flawed in structure. Some so much so that they really need to be round-filed. I cringe hearing how some of these writers have spent years penning their first novel (or perhaps even many subsequent ones), and often have spent additional years trying to get an agent to sign them. These are wasted years.

Sure, all that effort may have been a good learning experience—to a point. But I liken this to someone without any training being given a thousand airplane parts and then told to put it all together (maybe with a confusing four-page diagram) with the aim of ending up with a perfectly operational and beautiful aircraft. It'll never fly.

Some of those writers actually do spend hard hours studying novel structure. As I mentioned, they buy the best books, attend workshops and conferences, hire editors, and join critique groups. But they still suffer novel failure. Over and over I see the same essential problems plaguing manuscripts.

So what is the problem? Are they just not trying hard enough? Can only the smartest, most talented people write great novels?

Writers Need a Holistic Approach to Novel Building

No, I don't believe that. I believe just about anyone with the determination, a love of storytelling, a good imagination, a firm handle on language and composition, and a jar of "butt glue" (to keep one stuck in that chair and writing) can write a great novel. But I also feel there is a dearth of how-to books that really address the key problems new novelists face and find daunting.

Aspiring novelists can find hundreds of books that will teach them tips on how to write a great plot, develop believable characters, and craft catchy dialog. There are books that focus on just about every novel component, and writers could spend years studying these books and still not really grasp how to construct a novel. Why? Because so much of what is taught is about the tools of the trade, but not so much about how to construct the entire "house."

Just as building a house is a very complex undertaking, building a novel requires a similar holistic approach. When a builder looks at blueprints, he sees "the big picture." He has to understand every single aspect of the process and think ten steps ahead—that's how my builder husband puts it. When he looks at the foundation blueprints, he envisions how this will affect the task of hanging joists and laying out the roofline. When studying the details for the concrete forms, he'll check the rebar specs to make sure they are going to be the right thickness to support that second-story extension. That house will never be built right if the builder only tackles one task myopically at a time. *Every step of the way*, he must keep in mind the finished product and how it is slated to look. He has to consider how every single part of this construction process affects and informs all the others.

Get a Handle on the Big Picture

And this is exactly what a novelist must do as well, and what few (if any) writing craft books teach. For a writer to write a great novel that is constructed soundly, she must work with the "big picture." All the elements in a novel—plot, premise, theme, characters, etc.—must work holistically and fit together perfectly. Too often writers throw a bunch of materials together and grab random tools they little know how to use, then start hammering. The result is usually a disaster. What is most painful is when the foundation is seriously flawed—meaning the core concept itself just doesn't hold together. For then, everything that is built upon such a foundation cannot stand. The house will collapse. The novel will fail.

Writing a novel, therefore, is not easy, despite what some say (and usually it's the people who have never written one who say that). Many manuscripts I critique seem to be written off the top of the head, the scenes just thrown onto the page without forethought. So few novels seem to be actually *constructed*. Or if they are constructed, they are done faultily, doomed to failure (and often by the end of page 1).

Being a building contractor's wife, I've spent many long hours nailing siding according to blueprint nailing specifications and cutting two-by-fours carefully to the sixteenth of an inch in order for all the

3

studs to fit precisely in framing up a house, so the word *construction* has a rich and evocative meaning for me. As does the word *blueprint*. Any builder who attempts to construct a complex house without engineered plans would be rightly called a fool.

How Much Time Do You Want to Waste?

Of course, "building" a faulty novel won't endanger anyone's life (we hope), but it can sure be a lesson in frustration and aggravation, and a very big waste of time. That's not to say practicing writing is a waste of time; it's not.

But, well, it can be if there is no end to the means.

If you write randomly and learn nothing, does it really benefit you? Sure, exercises like participating in NaNoWriMo (National Novel Writing Month) teach you admirable things like discipline, perseverance, and stick-to-itiveness (yep, that really is a word!). But those qualities alone will not improve your writing skills or turn you into a novelist.

To use a different analogy, I could spend three hours pouring random ingredients into a big bowl and stirring, stirring, stirring. That doesn't guarantee that when I pour it into a pan and bake it, a delicious and beautiful cake will emerge from my oven.

Most novels I critique are a lot like that bowl of random elements. I don't mean to be harsh and insensitive. I know what it's like to write for months, thinking I was churning out a masterpiece—only to learn years later how utterly off track I was. Meaning, how uninformed I was about novel structure. Oh how I wish someone had taught me what I needed to know thirty years ago. Yes, I wasted a lot of time. And my aim in writing this book is to keep you from doing the same.

It's really hard to take a finished product like that yucky baked cake and turn it into something palatable, let alone delicious. If only writers took the time to find a solid, time-tested recipe and followed that. A recipe is like . . . a blueprint. Which brings me back around to building construction.

If you haven't figured me out yet, let me just say I am all about *not* wasting time. Life is short, too short. Some of you have read my polite rants on plotting and learning this craft well so as to *not* waste time. Time is the most precious and valuable commodity we have. It is a limited resource, and life demands we spend the increments of time on so many things. If we wrote down everything we did in a day, every

4

tiny little thing we did requiring a measure of time, we would probably be shocked. We have to divide up our time into little bits in order to take care of the many responsibilities we handle.

I'm not saying we should be neurotic and never waste a second. But why waste time if we don't need to? And when it comes to writing novels, I am astounded by how much time writers are willing to waste, basically stirring that bowl of ingredients day after day (and even year after year), without first taking the time to find the right recipe and then following the directions using the required ingredients.

I know I'm jumping back and forth here between baking a cake and building a house. But successful building and baking both center on careful preparation. Some of you can't relate to being on a construction crew and framing up a house. But most of you can relate to following a recipe and cooking something, right? Even if it's just one of those box cakes that state all you have to add are water, an egg, and a half-cup of oil. Simple, but you still need to do what it says—*basically*—or your cake will come out awful.

All in all, for just about every task we do in life, we follow some sort of instructions in order to succeed. Change the oil in your car. Upload a picture to Facebook. Follow a Google map to get to a place you've never been. So why is it so many writers think they don't need to follow instructions when constructing a novel?

Different Techniques but the Same Engineering Principles

Here's one reason: there are lots of different blueprints (or recipes) out there regarding novel construction. So many different techniques and styles. Some writers throw their hands up thinking that since that's the case, it really doesn't matter what method they use. Clearly anything goes. You take all those basic ingredients of plot, character, dialog, and theme and throw them into the mixer and, voila! A novel!

Well, here's the thing. If you ask great writing instructors about this, they will tell you there are time-tested rules or principles to novel building. Just as with constructing a house. There are myriads of houses—of different sizes, shapes, and layouts—many made of very different materials. But there are basic principles that tie in with the natural laws of physics and engineering. Materials have stress loads and limitations. Those factors have to be considered by the engineer designing the blueprints. And the building contractor has to follow those blueprints to ensure the house will be sturdy and safe.

In the same manner, novel construction requires acknowledging the scope, function, and limitations of all its elements. There are structures that have proven to be solid and others flawed. Regardless of genre, writer's style, or premise, there are some construction basics that apply to pretty much every novel—unless you are going with something experimental and you don't really care if the whole thing collapses. But most novelists want their novels to stand the test of time and stand up to the scrutiny of their target audience. They attempt to "build a house" their fans can inhabit and enjoy, which is the dwelling place of their story.

You can already see where this is leading to, I'm sure. My aim is to help you become a terrific builder and engineer, and by learning what these twelve essential pillars are and how they support your story, you will become proficient in novel construction. No more throwing a bunch of materials into the mixer and hoping a great book comes out. Novel construction doesn't have to be (and shouldn't be) guesswork.

By following established blueprints for novel construction, you can use your time wisely and write a terrific novel, while still having time to do all those other things you want and need to do in your life, including stopping to smell the roses and spending time with your family (remember them?).

So get ready to load up that tool belt with construction tools as we look deeply at the twelve key pillars of novel construction.

Chapter 1: Building Construction 101

Imagine your novel as a house. Or more like an ancient Greek building, such as the Parthenon. Made completely of marble, heavy marble—including the massive roof. Then imagine how strong those columns have to be to support such a gargantuan weight. One replacement column recently installed on the Parthenon weighed in at around fifty tons! Although no one has ever weighed the entire Parthenon, architects state that just the cast iron that supports the dome of the US Capitol building in Washington, DC, has been estimated at around 8.9 *million* pounds. It's hard to believe any structure made of any materials could hold up such weight.

But these buildings have remained standing through centuries, without collapsing, which attests to the strength and reliability of the materials used in these structures—as well as the brilliance of the architects who designed them.

Novelists are architects too—architects of story. Just as a level, appropriate, and rock-solid foundation is needed as a base to any lasting building, a writer must have a similarly strong and informed foundation in order to write strong novels. Upon such a foundation a great novel can be built. But as much as the right foundation is essential, the structural integrity of the entire project must be exact or the "building" will collapse.

So if we liken the completed novel to the roof—the very heavy marble roof—then consider the pillars supporting the roof as the key to success. We want "fifty-ton" columns to support our roof so it will not only look sturdy but also stand the test of time.

Not Just Pretty to Look At

Aesthetics are a main concern in construction. Architects are praised for designing a beautiful, captivating house or monument. But structural integrity cannot be sacrificed on the altar of beauty. They go hand in hand. I've always thought it a shame that those exquisitely crafted ice or sand sculptures I've seen constructed as entries in a competition were so temporal. One wave . . . or one day in a warm room . . . and those magnificent works of art disappeared. Although I understand the joy experienced in the act of creating, it seems a waste to put that much effort out to create something so beautiful and detailed, only to watch it melt before your eyes.

Some novels are like those ephemeral sculptures—adorned with lovely writing, an intriguing premise, and perfectly edited to present the appearance of a great novel. But when examined under the scrutiny of a "construction engineer" (read: savvy reader or critical literary agent), the pillars that support the story are shown to be flimsy and weak. Collapse is inevitable—and probably has already occurred—even in the first few pages. And the sad thing is the writer can't see it. Or upon learning the story has collapsed, she can't understand how in the world that could have happened.

She might say, "But I had a great idea. I worked out a clever, fresh plot. I have great characters. So what went wrong?"

Take the Requisite Construction Course

I'm married to a building contractor, who is a stickler for structure. He pores endlessly over blueprints before beginning to construct a house, often finding mistakes the engineers have made. He understands structure so well that he can spot any little thing that might compromise the support of the house. It could be a prescribed nail pattern for a sheer wall, or the thickness of the rebar specified to be used in the concrete forms. This type of knowledge and deep understanding of construction is not something that can be learned by watching a few TV shows or skimming through some do-it-yourself books found at The Home Depot. A lot of this kind of knowledge comes from on-the-job experience, which is mostly how my husband learned his skills—assisting, watching, and questioning the expert building contractors he worked with for years. Hands-on experience coupled with diligent "book" learning make for a sound education.

And so too writers, to construct solid, lasting novels, need both "hands-on" experience and "book" learning. I use the term "book learning" as a catch-all for any type of informational instruction that is not a part of actual practice—which is sitting down and writing. This can be knowledge gained by attending workshops (online or in person), conferences, and writing retreats; reading blog posts and articles on writing; studying writing craft books; and working with writing groups and critique partners.

Don't Be a Tinkerer

A lot of writers are like weekend handymen. Once they've gotten a little bit of knowledge, skill, and writing time under their belt, they feel they're ready for the big time. But many inexperienced handymen (or women) tackle a repair or remodel project only to meet with disaster.

I'm reminded of the commercial showing a man trying to fix his light switch in the bathroom, but when he flips the switch, the toilet flushes (which actually would take some pretty clever planning and construction to achieve). My husband is never happy when I tinker with things I really am not qualified to mess with. He knows that no matter how determined or careful I am, I'm being foolish and counterproductive by attempting to fix something I haven't adequately learned how to fix.

This doesn't mean I'm stupid; with proper knowledge and some practice, I'm sure I could take that sink apart, unclog the drain, and put it all back together again without flooding my kitchen. And that would be a good skill for me to learn (but since I'm married to such a handy guy who actually likes doing repairs like that, I haven't bothered). However, a novelist doesn't have the handy guy or gal at his beck and call to come running to fix everything while he's writing his novel. The novelist, as sole architect, builder, and decorator (unless doing a collaborative novel), has to have all the chops needed to construct that great novel.

It wouldn't do to throw your hands up a few pages into the writing and turn the project over to someone else to fix. If you want to be a proficient builder of lasting, terrific stories, you need to take Construction 101. And that is what this book will do—give you the requisite course in how to structure a novel that, hopefully, will remain unscathed by both the ravages of time and critics.

9

Sure, You Can Break the Rules

Although every novel is unique (one hopes), regardless of genre, writing style, or story line, each faces the same construction issues. Like the laws of physics and gravity, the basic supports of good novel construction apply to every novel—unless of course you want to get wild and crazy and go for the experimental method. And I'm not saying that's wrong or invalid. I support creativity on plenty of levels—and so do various audiences in the world that are open and eager to embrace such creativity. A lot of literary fiction breaks many of the "rules" of time-tested and proven novel structure. And many are hailed as great works of literature. So, please don't think I'm saying that if you don't follow this "construction course," you do so at your peril. Just know that, as in building, when you "wing it" or experiment with unusual materials (such as substituting Silly Putty for cement or duct tape for Simpson ties), your finished product might not hold up when that flood or tornado hits.

There's a reason building codes exist and why contractors are required to follow them before they can pass their inspections and get the project signed off by the building inspector. Many of these codes ensure the house or building will be safe to inhabit, and that the structural support has been built to specs given by the highly trained (we hope) engineer who made the blueprints.

Of course, if a novel flops from faulty "materials," it's not likely anyone's life will be endangered. Maybe there'll be a resultant bruised ego, or maybe not. But if a novelist really does want to have the greatest chance of success—and I don't mean success in the monetary or worldly sense—she needs to get some basic construction skills under her belt.

Building a house with excellently engineered blueprints makes the project go so much more smoothly than trying to build a house with faulty plans—or plans missing pages. A conscientious builder will not begin construction unless he has all the blueprints he needs, which cover everything from plumbing to trusses to siding to roofing. He chooses only the best materials and is careful to follow the plans. And when he does so, the result is a well-constructed, solid house that looks exactly as he expected it to look—and that is perfectly safe and functional so the new homeowners can move in without worrying they'll be crushed in their sleep by a collapsed roof.

I sleep well at night, not at all worried my roof is going to fall on me. I didn't build this house I live in, but I know a licensed contractor did, and he had to pass all the inspections before the house was allowed to be put up for sale. This gives me peace of mind. And novelists can experience a similar peace of mind when they "build" their novel following the structural principles that have been "approved" by most building inspectors. They can avoid a lot of frustration and heartache caused by endlessly rewriting and tinkering with a novel that was not correctly constructed from the start.

Why suffer such aggravation and waste so much time trying to guess how to make your novel better and fix all the many nebulous problems inherent in your story—which you know are there but have no idea how to resolve? A little knowledge goes a long way . . . and a *lot* of knowledge goes a *really* long way.

So don't try to cram by flipping through a few how-to books and reading a couple of articles. Becoming adept at any difficult skill takes hard work and practice. You need that hands-on experience and the "book" learning to become a great novelist. But the good thing about taking "Construction 101" is this: not only can you use this knowledge every time you sit down to write a novel, you can also take on any project your heart desires and be confident you can build a strong, sturdy novel that will have lasting power

Chapter 2: Introduction to the 12 Key Pillars

Grab a seat and open your notebook—or the workbook, if you've obtained one. Get prepared to become a building contractor. And remember—it's all about structural support. To make it simple and easy for you, I've organized your building course into twelve sections, or twelve pillars. These are the twelve essential pillars that will "hold up" your novel. In order to take much of the mystery and confusion out of novel building, I came up with this straightforward and practical approach, organizing the requisite components of a novel into something easy to conceptualize and work with.

We'll look at the four primary corner pillars first—likened to the important corner supports of a building—for they provide the main framework upon which your entire story rests. These are essential to get right. And once you have those four support pillars in place, you can play around with the other eight. Those eight secondary pillars add the additional strength needed to hold up the novel, and their "size and weight" in your novel may vary depending on your concept, genre, and other considerations. Once a writer sets in place the four solid corner pillars, the other eight can be fashioned and positioned. But without those four major supports, the entire structure will collapse.

Since these four corner pillars are the big supports of your story, we'll be spending the most time on them. These are what I see lacking in many of the novels I critique and usually are the primary cause of construction failure. A novel that ignores or belittles the importance of any of these four pillars will be doomed to fail—every time:

- **Concept with a Kicker**
- **Conflict with High Stakes**
- **Protagonist with a Goal**
- **Theme with a Heart**

The eight secondary pillars provide additional support to your story, and they are developed after the four corner pillars are built:

- **Plot and Subplots in a String of Scenes**
- **Secondary Characters with Their Own Needs**
- **Setting with a Purpose**
- **Tension Ramped to the Max**
- **Dialog—Compressed and Essential**
- **Voice—Unique for Each Character**
- **Writing Style—Concise and Specific**
- **Motifs for Cohesion and Depth**

You Have to Pass Every Inspection

Builders are required to pass numerous inspections before any house they're building can ultimately get "signed off." If anywhere along the line an inspector finds something wrong—not up to code or otherwise in conflict with the blueprints—the builder has to fix it in order to pass inspection.

So here's the fun part! With each of the twelve pillars you will get an inspection checklist of twelve sets of essential questions. These are questions you will ask yourself about your novel and must be answered solidly to ensure you have a strong pillar. I'll provide checklists that you can photocopy, as well as give you downloadable links to the PDFs, so you can print them out (as often as needed) to use as worksheets to help you firm up your pillars.

By the end of this book you'll have 12 checklists, with a total of 144 sets of questions. By answering all those key questions, you will know you have built well. If you're stumped on some of them, that will show you what you need help on, and you can then ask an editor or writing coach specifics in order to get the answers you need. These checklists are great tools you can use on each and every novel you construct, regardless of genre!

I can promise you—if you pass your inspections with flying colors, you will have a finished novel you can be proud of and that will stand up under the weight of scrutiny. No, you may not please every reader, for there's no accounting for taste, right? But you can be sure that regardless of who walks through your house—or sleeps in the bedroom—that your roof will stay put and your house will remain standing firm through any fire, flood, or tornado that might attack it.

So let's get started!

Part 1: The Four Essential Corner Pillars of Novel Construction

Pillar #1: Concept with a Kicker

Chapter 3: Idea, Premise, and Concept

We're going to be spending the bulk of this book looking at what I call "the four corner pillars" of novel construction. While there is no set order to any of these pillars, I've already mentioned that these primary four need to be solid before you focus on the other eight. Your roof [read: novel] will collapse if any of these corner supports fail, so instead of working on your novel using a shotgun approach or trying to tackle the components in a random fashion, do what builders do—frame up the building with the required supporting beams before even thinking about putting on the roof or laying down flooring.

In the last chapters of the book, I'll be showing you ways you can holistically brainstorm these four pillars together, growing your ideas and developing them so that the pillars are tightly connected. This is a different way to approach novel writing, but one I think you will soon learn is the most effective and intuitive.

I listed the four main supports in the last chapter: Concept with a Kicker, Conflict with High Stakes, Protagonist with a Goal, and Theme with a Heart. Even though you haven't yet learned the nuances and attributes for the other three pillars, throughout these initial chapters, as we go deep into these four primary novel supports, I will continually draw your attention to them, for these corner pillars need to be solidly constructed—which can only be done if you work on all four together.

Think how a building would need those four pillars already built and equal in size, shape, width, and weight when they are put into place. That's what you'll need to do before you can construct the remaining eight pillars.

So let's take an initial look at the first pillar—Concept with a Kicker, which is often the most difficult one to get a handle on, and is the weakest pillar in most novels.

More Than a Good Idea

Let me start by getting this notion of *concept* simmering in your head. Concept seems to be hard for novelists to understand. Granted, a concept, by definition, is an idea, thought, or notion. And some excellent writing instructors differentiate between idea, concept, and premise. I find the terms a bit confusing, though—especially when used to mean different things. So I'm going to keep it simple.

Every great novel starts with a basic idea. An idea for a story. You could phrase an idea by starting with "What if . . . ?" What if a comet was about to crash into Earth and scientists had to find a way to destroy it? What if a man on death row was innocent and only one person believed him? What if a woman fell in love with a man and it turned out he was her brother? Writers generate innumerable ideas for stories, and many ideas they come up with have a germ of potential—the potential to be turned into a truly great novel. Every great novel, in the beginning, started with some *idea*.

Ideas Are a Dime a Dozen

But, a great idea does not make a novel. Some ideas are fine for a short story, but they don't have the "legs" to be fashioned into a lengthy novel. Almost all ideas fall way too short of novel potential. Well, how can you determine what has legs and what doesn't?

It's only when ideas are developed into a "Concept with a Kicker" that they start to have the potential to be worked into a novel. Think about a lump of clay. That's your idea. That lump of clay is *not* a beautiful vase. It's just a lump of potential. That is what your good idea is. We all have a lot of lumps on the table, but they are not going to turn into vases by sitting there. You are going to have to work on them to get them into shape.

So in this way, ideas need to be taken to a higher level; they have to have a kicker. Ideas are a dime a dozen. Maybe even two dozen.

17

I came up with this phrase "Concept with a Kicker" because I wanted some simple way to roll all the diverse and confusing information about concept, premise, plot, and idea into one clear statement.

Well, what is a kicker? To me, it is the very specific, unique "shape" that idea is going to take on. The kicker takes the blah lump of clay and turns it into a stunning vase. Or sculpture. Or whatever you have in mind as the finished product.

So, just how in the world do you take an idea and infuse it with a kicker? The secret is tied up with the other three corner pillars. We'll get into that shortly.

What's a Premise?

As I just stated, a writer may have a good idea. And maybe he's formed that idea into a premise of sorts. All that means is he's come up with that "what if?" question that supposes something will happen if a certain situation is established.

For example, an idea for the story might be: "What if an 'ordinary guy' has the task of destroying a ring of power?" What turns the idea into a *premise* is the supposition that something *prompts the need for the task to be accomplished*: "An evil power searches for a ring that's been lost for ages, and *in order to prevent him from taking over the world*, that ring must be destroyed."

That's a premise. A premise *proposes* or presumes something, and what follows supports that premise. In the example of *The Lord of the Rings* (above), the premise presumes there is an evil power that wants the ring, and so the plot is tied up with dealing with that situation.

You could say, for example: "I propose this (bad, scary, tense) situation, and this is what must be done to deal with it." As you might conclude, a lot of ideas fail even at this "premise" stage by not having a compelling situation that requires some specific action. This is where premise meets Protagonist with a Goal, Conflict with High Stakes, and Theme with a Heart. Someone with some passion needs to deal with the situation in the midst of huge conflict.

It Has to Be Compelling

Note I used the word *compelling*. You might have a nice idea for a story, one that presumes a situation (premise) that calls for a character

18

to act or respond. Yet, if I told you I planned to write a futuristic novel about a man who gets hired to invent a machine, is paid a fortune to do so, and then agrees to have his memory wiped, how compelling a story would that be in itself? Not very. With that idea alone, I have little-to-no compelling story. The premise is he's offered a job and he takes it, and his employer wants to keep the invention top secret, even from the inventor. That's not much of a scenario. But when you take that idea and add the kicker, the idea is jettisoned into the realm of viable concept.

Just what is the kicker in the movie *Paycheck*? The protagonist, Michael Jennings, finishes the job he's been hired to do, and discovers to his horror, after his memory's been wiped of those three years, that he turned down the ninety million dollars he earned and left himself a manila envelope of strange, unrelated simple objects. Something happened during those three years spent working for this company—something so serious that he was willing to give up the money that would have allowed him to retire in great comfort. Quickly, viewers see this kicker in action as Jennings is chased and his life is thrust into danger with enemies trying to stop him from doing something that he knows he must do—whatever that is. The clues are in that envelope, and what unfolds is a tense, gripping story of high concept.

Don't Get Wrapped Up in the Terms

You don't have to scratch your head trying to figure out which threads belong to premise and which to idea. Just know that to have a Concept with a Kicker, you have to tie in the other three essential corner pillars—Conflict with High Stakes, Protagonist with a Goal, and Theme with a Heart. If you construct all four of these pillars together, your idea will become a strong Concept with a Kicker. But without even one of them, you will only have an idea or a premise at best. And a great novel *must* have a Concept with a Kicker.

Writers flounder trying to figure out how to make their idea compelling so that they will have a great novel. Unfortunately, too many search for this "secret" or magic to take place while writing the novel, hoping it will just develop on its own or appear organically as the story unfolds. Let me say simply, "It won't." It has to be carefully constructed.

I might be so bold as to say that you could take just about any idea, even if it's pretty lame, and turn it into a terrific concept if you come up with a great kicker. So let's take a long look at what a kicker is.

Chapter 4: Concept with a Kicker

So what is a kicker? Just to be clear here: a kicker isn't the same thing as a plot twist. Plot twists are "kickers" in their own right—meaning they are surprising turns or reveals in a story, and, as such, they "kick" the plot into high gear. Some novels have a great plot twist at the end, like Jodi Picoult's best seller *My Sister's Keeper*. The plot twist is so intense and unexpected, it evokes a lot of emotion from many readers. I thought it was a terrific twist, but some of my friends hated it. Without doing a spoiler here, Picoult masterfully created a shocking ending to this very heavy drama.

Yet, the twisty ending wasn't the kicker. A novel can't ride four hundred pages on a kicker in the last chapter. And likewise—if you have a plot twist early on in the book, if it's just a simple plot twist, it won't give the novel "legs" to last the entire read.

In *My Sister's Keeper*, Picoult creates a great kicker. This is the story of a girl named Anna, who is conceived for one purpose: to be a donor for her older sister, Kate, who has leukemia. That, in itself, is quite a kicker, for it brings to mind all kinds of conflict (resentment, jealousy, anger, etc.). Remember what a premise is? It proposes a situation that requires action. This novel is a perfect example. A girl with leukemia needs a donor, and the best choice would be one who is blood related and as closely compatible as possible.

But Picoult kicks her idea even higher by centering the book on the plot element of Anna seeking legal action against her parents to prevent them from forcing her to be a donor. Now look at how the stakes have been raised (which is part of the pillar "Conflict with High Stakes"). Anna's actions can now endanger Kate's life, as well as cause a painful rift between her and her parents. And deeply embedded in this kicker is yet another one—which has to do with how Kate feels about both her illness and her sister's role as her blood and bone marrow donor.

Plot Twists Are Not "Concept Kickers"

Think about the blockbuster movie *The Planet of the Apes*. Do you recall the great twist/surprise kicker at the end, showing Commander Taylor (played by Charlton Heston) coming upon the half-buried Statue of Liberty and realizing, to his horror, that he is on Earth and not some other planet? That's a great moment. But if the movie failed to have a great Concept with a Kicker all the way through, no one would have stayed in the theater long enough to see that ending.

What is the Concept with a Kicker for the movie? I would say it is something like this: "An astronaut lands on a planet run by intelligent apes that enslave humans—who are the unintelligent animals. Taylor's intelligence threatens to destroy the apes' entire way of life and worldview, and so they do whatever they must to stop him from reaching his goal (which is to escape)." The movie as a whole is *not* about the twist at the end; it's about the problem created by the situation and what the hero must do to remedy it and reach his goal (Note how strong this pillar—Protagonist with a Goal—is in this story). The secret of the apes' past is an important plot element in the movie that drives the story and tension (huge Conflict with High Stakes), but it's not the core of the concept. Theme with a Heart? At the core of this concept lie many themes: the definition of humanity, oppression of the weak, the inhumane treatment of animals, and even a look at racism (in symbolism).

In a similar way, the Concept with a Kicker for *The Sixth Sense* is not wrapped up in the fact that Dr. Malcolm Crowe realizes, to his shock, that he is actually dead. That is a brilliant plot twist, and certainly is foundational to the plot. But just what makes that movie so compelling—all the way up to where we actually see the scene in which Malcolm has his moment of realization?

The story concept has a great kicker. It's about a therapist racked by the guilt of failure and seeking personal redemption through helping a very disturbed boy who can "see dead people." He thinks that by helping young Cole he will find peace (his spiritual/emotional goal tied in with his plot goal), and by using his skills as a therapist, he succeeds in both reaching his goal and in helping "cure" Cole. The playing out of this concept is fascinating, and even without the twist it would be a strong story.

Writer/director of *The Sixth* Sense, M. Night Shyamalan, uses a similar technique with *Unbreakable* and *Signs*. Both these movies have surprising plot twists near the end, but the concept for each has a great kicker that supports the whole story. Both are about rich characters driven by extreme need and passion and going after a specific goal, while facing tough inner and outer conflict along the way. His themes are huge and powerful in these stories. Being a very character-driven writer, I find that the most successful element in stories like these are the characters, whose core needs and passions are intrinsically woven into the concept of the story. And often the inner conflict has higher stakes than the outer ones, but conflict is found in spades.

Which is the point I'm trying to emphasize in these opening chapters on the four corner pillars. Concept cannot be just about plot. A great concept for a novel can't hold up if it's just a good idea or an interesting premise. It has to have the support of the three other pillars. That's when the concept gets into high gear with a kicker.

You Don't Need a Wholly Original Basic Idea

You've probably heard it said there are only so many basic plot ideas, and that's true. Every general plot for a novel has been done many times over. And many terrific novels are just variations on the same old story. So, if it's not *required* to come up with a wholly unique plot that no one else has ever done, how can a general idea get turned into a Concept with a Kicker?

By tweaking the norm or expected. Bring to that tired old plot idea something unexpected, something intriguing—some factor or component that will shake the traditional, basic, simplistic story and make it a Concept with a Kicker.

Let's say you want to write a romance. A very basic, formulaic-style of romance. You might choose a subgenre, such as paranormal, historical, or young adult. It doesn't matter which. But with each genre and subgenre, there are traditional story lines—predictable scenarios. And there is nothing wrong with that. You could grab any number of those "boiler plate" romances and create a great novel so long as your concept has a kicker.

I write historical Western romance novels. I must have watched hundreds of Western movies and TV shows during my lifetime. I'm now reading a whole lot of Western novels—traditional or classic novels, as well as romance stories. I can easily attest that the "same old" stories are done repeatedly. There are plenty of remakes of the great Westerns as well. There must be a few dozen movies that are about some woman widowed and trying to run a ranch or homestead who needs help or protection from some strong, honorable cowboy to stave off the bad guy in town (who is usually mean, rich, and powerful—and always seems to be dressed completely in black) who wants her land.

But many of these are truly great stories because they have a compelling enough "what if?" question and enough of a tweak on the basic story to add that interest. They may have the same kind of strong protagonist with a great goal, high stakes, strong conflict, and some theme or two at the heart (usually something to do with justice or vengeance).

Tweak Your Basic Idea to Give It Unexpected Flair

There are lots of ways to tweak your idea to move it into Concept with a Kicker. Here are just a few ways:

- *Setting*: Boy meets girl, boy hates girl, boy falls in love with girl . . . in an elevator during a power outage. Or while trying to steal the *Mona Lisa* and escape. Or while walking a tightrope across two skyscrapers. Or when wandering lost across the Alaskan tundra. By choosing an unusual setting for your idea, you might find ways of ramping up the conflict and stakes; giving your protagonist a stronger, more intriguing goal; or bringing out deeper, richer themes.

  Think about your themes, what you really want your book to be about (which we will explore in depth later). A theme of legal justice might give you the idea of setting your love story in a prison, between a warden and a convicted murderer. A theme of forgiveness could pit a mother of an accidentally killed child in court falling in love with the drunk driver who killed that child.

  Setting in itself can generate all kinds of conflict and high stakes. What if you placed your characters at an archaeological dig site, or in the middle of a wilderness rescue, or shipwrecked in the middle of the Pacific Ocean? By brainstorming ideas for setting, you might find just the perfect place to stage your novel that will help turn your good idea into a great Concept with a Kicker.

- *Career*: Writers often cast characters in boring vocations. Of course, your genre may have some sway in this (you couldn't have an unmarried woman in Victorian England be a chief detective . . . or could you?), but try to think outside the envelope. Take the idea you have for your protagonist and see how that looks when you make her an astronaut, a nuclear physicist working to create an invisible force field, or a paranormal healer that can see people's illnesses in their eyes. Buffy the vampire slayer wasn't some tough Xena warrior. She was a cute blond high school student (until she graduated and went on to college).

The movie *Dragonfly* is a paranormal story about a dead wife trying to communicate with her grieving husband. What brings a kicker to this concept is that both are/were doctors, and the wife sends messages through the terminally ill children she cared for in the hospital. Choosing this medical profession for the main character helped add conflict to the story, for this doctor appeared crazy to believe his wife was reaching out to him from the netherworld, and it created a terrific scenario for how and why she died. Play around with vocations and see if you can take your concept to a higher place by choosing something unexpected.

- *World Events*: What if you take your simple romance story and set it during the 9/11 disaster in New York City? Or on a tropical beach when the biggest tsunami struck? Or in Dallas the day JFK was shot? The movie *Titanic* was a basic formula romance that could have been set anywhere at any time, but how could any stakes and conflict be greater than this? Natural disasters and impacting world or local events might be just the factor you need to ramp up your concept.

Caveat: don't choose a random setting or career or event just because it is unusual. Every choice you make for your novel has to have a specific purpose. You don't want to build your pillar with marbles and molasses just because it looks neat. That pillar won't hold up anything. Think about the heart of your story, what it's really about (which is theme), then come up with setting, career, and scenarios that will best serve the interests of your premise and concept. And these aren't the only ways you can tweak an idea to make it zing with concept. Characters' hobbies, passions, past hurts, secrets, and unusual upbringings—the possibilities are only limited by your imagination.

Remember: Concept with a Kicker is an idea taken to a higher level. It's about coming up with a great "what if?" and framing that premise in an intriguing way that brings into play conflict that has high stakes, a protagonist with a compelling goal, and a theme with heart.

Nailing Concept with a Kicker

Here's a fun thing you can do. Go to IMDb.com (Internet Movie Database) and type in the names of some movies you're familiar with. Or highlight the tab for movies, then click on the link for "popular movies" or "Oscar winners" or "Top 250." Or if you write in a particular genre, choose that genre and go through some of those movie blurbs. Each movie you click on will give you a short blurb (elevator pitch, essentially) that tells you the concept and the kicker. Go through a couple of dozen movie blurbs and see if you can pull out the idea, then identify the kicker. What you're going to see overall is a brief summary of the movie, but the key element of what makes it an interesting concept is usually noted.

I'll grab a random few currently under "Top 250" (chosen by votes on their website) and examine these.

Remember, as I mentioned earlier, building a novel is a holistic endeavor, so the sooner you start looking at the "bigger picture" of a story's structure, the sooner you'll become a proficient novel builder. Pay attention to how these other corner pillars show up intrinsically in these stories. With each of these examples, we're going to look at the Protagonist with a Goal, Conflict with High Stakes, and Theme with a Heart as well as the Concept with a Kicker. This is your "four-pack" that you need to hard-wire into your brain. And once you do, you will be able to take any idea and see the potential for it to be fashioned (or not) into a great novel concept.

So let's look at these movie blurbs with this holistic approach.

The Shawshank Redemption

The Shawshank Redemption is one of my favorite movies, and is also clearly a favorite of many, since it's #1 on the list. Here's the blurb for the movie: "Two imprisoned men bond over a number of years, finding solace and eventual redemption through acts of common decency." Wow, no kicker here at all, right? This is just an idea. The premise might be molded into this question: "What if a man wrongly convicted of murdering his wife has to spend years in prison and find a way to survive (and escape)?" The bit about the "acts of common decency" gives a hint at the kicker, and speaks to the heart of the themes in this story.

Since this movie doesn't seem to have a kicker (or does it?), how is it possible it's one of the all-time great movies? Is it just because of the terrific acting and compelling characters?

If I broke this movie down into the four corner pillars, it would be easy to see how strong the other three are: *Protagonist with a Goal*: Yep, Andy Dufresne wants desperately to get out of jail. That's a huge goal. *Conflict with High Stakes*: He has to deal with all the evil men in prison, including the warden, who terrorizes his life. Huge stakes. Plus, his plan to escape brings high stakes, for if he's caught, not only will he never get the chance to get out ever again, he'll probably be beaten to death or close to it.

Theme with a Heart: Lots of themes run through this movie, and they are powerful. Red, his closest friend and the narrator of the story, tells Andy something that is a repeated motif: "Get busy living or get busy dying." Themes of not giving up, and justice and revenge, are strong in this story. And the movie ends with a beautiful bit about hope, which as the key theme at the heart of this movie. Andy tells Red, "Hope is a good thing, maybe the best of things, and no good thing ever dies." That's wrapping up a story with a big thematic "wow!"

So what about our Concept with a Kicker? What's the kicker in *The Shawshank Redemption*? I would have to say it is this: A mild, gentle banker serving time in Shawshank Prison in the 1940s for a crime he didn't commit concocts a fantastic and unbelievable way to not only escape the impossible-to-escape prison but bring to justice the corrupt individuals running the prison at the same time."

The story isn't just about Andy's escape. Escaping from prison is a great *idea* and offers a lot of potential for a strong story—if there's a kicker and the other three pillars are strong. *Shawshank* is compelling due to the impossibility of Andy's predicament and his mild, unassuming nature and slight build, which makes him the least likely candidate to escape.

And he doesn't just escape. His orchestrating all the pieces needed to accomplish justice is the added component to the plot that makes this more than a "prison escape" movie.

Remember the blurb about two men finding solace and redemption through acts of common decency? The protagonist doesn't just save himself, he saves Red—and not just by helping him once he gets out of prison. He helps Red find that inner redemption and peace that he never knew he could achieve. Dufresne's time in prison changes many lives in a powerful way, and that's part of the kicker, for no one would have ever expected such a man to have that kind of impact on this hostile environment.

The Prestige

The Prestige is a fascinating story about two magicians who live in the same city at the end of the nineteenth century. Here's the blurb: "Rival magicians in turn-of-the-century London battle each other for trade secrets. However, their friendly competition evolves into a bitter rivalry making them fierce enemies-for-life and consequently jeopardizing the lives of everyone around them." An intriguing scenario and not the usual cast of characters make this idea appealing.

Remember how I talked about choosing an interesting career to give a twist to a simple story? Here's a great example of an intriguing career—and setting. By setting this story a hundred-plus years in the past, it makes the "tech" developed in the story fascinating and magical. (The same story could also have been worked into a futuristic setting, to give a more scientific tweak to the invention, but the absence of technology back then enhances the mystery of the story.)

The movie features a protagonist, Robert Angier, with a strong goal—to uncover the secrets of the other magician's—a man Angier blames for his beloved wife's death years earlier. This rivalry is at the heart of the kicker. Like many movies, there is a terrific plot twist later on in the movie, but remember—a plot twist is not a kicker. This plot twist involving a strange machine—which accounts for the rival's seemingly impossible magic tricks—adds great interest to the story. But as mentioned earlier in this chapter, a concept's kicker has to be less specific than a singular plot element or twist and more overarching as far as the concept goes.

So what is the kicker in *The Prestige*? It's found in the intensity of the two men's rivalry. It's about the way their bitter rivalry "jeopardizes the lives of everyone around them." It's not just a story about two magicians seeking to outshine each other (idea). It's about this passionate, personal rivalry that is the strong force underlying the protagonist's motivation.

Such a kicker has the potential to move the magicians' skills from entertainment to revenge and murder. A unique concept that adds intrigue.

Yet, in order for this movie idea to be developed into a terrific story, the other three story pillars have to be strongly entwined with the concept and kicker. The protagonist is driven by his grief toward his goal. The stakes are high because many lives are at risk, and the themes of love and revenge and (lack of) forgiveness are strongly woven in.

I hope you are starting to get an idea of how the four story components support one another. None can stand alone. Take one out of a story, and it just won't hold up—whether it's a novel, film, or play.

12 Angry Men

12 Angry Men is an old classic film (1957) that is still a favorite. If you haven't seen the movie, I highly recommend it. This is the blurb: "A dissenting juror in a murder trial slowly manages to convince the others that the case is not as obviously clear as it seemed in court." The kicker is pretty obvious here. It's not just the story of a trial or a jury attending a famous trial. It's a story about eleven men who want a guilty verdict, who gradually, one by one, have their fixed opinions changed by just one man who believes in the accused party's innocence.

This is a fascinating kicker. The movie is a deep study of many themes, looking at how we are quick and eager to judge, and so brings into the story issues of mercy, fairness, racism, and justice. The protagonist has a strong goal—do all he can to convince the other eleven jurors the man is not guilty. The stakes are high, of course. Not just for the defendant but for the jurors—for they have to live with the burden of their decision—which is what the protagonist drives home to these men.

It makes me think of the novel *The Runaway Jury* by John Grisham, which was also made into a movie. This story has it all: a great protagonist with a killer goal (actually two protagonists—Nicholas and Marlee, boyfriend/girlfriend)—to get on a jury (but not just any jury). The themes are huge, and the conflict and stakes explode out the roof.

The *idea*—two young adults try to sway a jury to get a particular outcome—might not be all that interesting. But when you tweak it, adding strong pillars of support, you have a Concept with a Kicker: two young adults bent on revenge and justice take on a high-powered lawyer named Fitch by weaseling into a jury in order to control the outcome. Their dangerous game escalates with Fitch's career and reputation on the line, as he races to uncover their secret past and agenda in order to stop them before it's too late.

Kickers Will Vary Based on Genre

You might argue that some novels really don't need a kicker. Maybe you write formulaic romantic suspense or cozy mysteries or traditional Westerns. Does that mean you don't need a kicker? You may not need much of one to sell books, but if you want to write a great story, one that will stand the test of time and be memorable, you'll want to infuse your basic plot with a kicker.

It doesn't have to be monumental, but it's not hard to take a good idea and make it a great one with a kicker. As we've gone over, sometimes all that is needed to turn an idea into a viable novel concept with "legs" is to create an intriguing framework in which to set your story.

Is a Kicker the Same as "High Concept"?

Hmm, maybe this "kicker" definition is a little hard to pinpoint. It makes me think of "high concept"—a term you may be familiar with. Here's how *Wikipedia* defines high concept: "High concept is a term used to refer to an artistic work that can be easily pitched with a succinctly stated premise. It can be contrasted with low concept, which is more concerned with character development and other subtleties that aren't as easily summarized. The origin of the term is in dispute." Well, that's a bit vague.

Michael Hauge, Hollywood screenwriting consultant, gives this definition as it pertains to movies (however, this applies agreeably to novels as well): "A high concept is a story concept that is strong enough that it will draw an audience without any other components. It is not dependent on casting, name director, execution, good word of mouth . . . it is simply the story idea alone that will promise an emotional experience."

One person defined "high concept" this way: "You tell me your amazing pitch for your book, and then I decide I have to kill you so I can steal your idea." Well, it's funny, but quite to the point. We're talking *big* idea. Just how intriguing is your concept or idea?

Think about a novel (series) like *The Hunger Games*. If all Suzanne Collins came up with was "a girl in an oppressive dystopic future society has to struggle to survive (and gets caught in a love triangle)," do you think she would have sold that book to a publisher? If the kicker—the premise of the games themselves—was not a part of the book(s), she might have had a good idea and maybe could have sold a few copies—but perhaps not millions.

The kicker in that novel was a fascinating predicament. Featuring a game that forced children to murder one another, Collins introduced an element into the primary structure (pillar) that could support the entire novel. Again, this is not just an idea or premise or plot point of a novel. This is a foundational concept that creates tension, mystery, keen interest, and curiosity. It makes readers ask questions they really want the answers for. How in the world could a child make it out alive? What kind of emotional damage would these children suffer? How could people stand to live in a world like this, and what would it take to stop this insanity?

Kickers make readers ask questions they want answered. Kickers move the ordinary into the extraordinary. Kickers take ordinary ideas and put them on steroids. Wouldn't we all want someone, albeit jokingly, to say to us: "Wow, that is such a kicker, I'm going to have to kill you so I can steal your idea and write that book myself"?

Yep, Another Caveat

Okay, you're right. I'll concede this point: not all novels have to have a *high-concept* kicker. If you are writing formula romance for

Harlequin's Love Inspired series, you may not need anything that outstanding. Same with a post-modern literary work—although I may pose the challenge that with every novel, a writer should be able to come up with a kicker of some sort. Even a baby one.

Some readers want to read the same kind of book over and over. Some publishers want to publish the same kind of story over and over (because of those readers willing and eager to buy those same stories again and again). And that's all well and good.

But I'm all about writing great stories—ones that will stand the test of time, like a sturdily built house. Yes, well-built romance novels written to formula are structured for success. And many will endure the ravages of time. Formulaic novels follow "building codes" and are a fine example of a builder using a blueprint correctly to build a specific kind of structure.

But if you are striking out "on your own" to create an original novel with a high concept, you'll need a great kicker.

Brainstorm Key Questions

So when you're brainstorming your ideas and homing in on the one you want to develop into your next novel, *or* if you're already writing a novel but feel it's not all that extraordinary, spend some time thinking about the kicker.

Here are some of the questions you want to ask, and some that will be on your "inspection checklist." These should get your creative juices stirring.

- What is unique and compelling about my central idea for my novel?

- How can I tweak this idea and infuse it with something outrageous, tense, full of conflict?

- Can I elevate the stakes dramatically for my main character to give the concept heightened drama and suspense? (Think of *The Hunger Games* and the element of death/murder.)

- What kind of goal can I give my main character that will seem impossible to reach?

- What controversial or sensitive issues or themes can be at the core of this idea so that it will tug on readers' hearts?

- How can I twist the whole idea so that it poses an intriguing dilemma or conflict?

Notice here I've brought in the other three key corner pillars—Protagonist with a Goal, Conflict with High Stakes, and Theme with a Heart. I mentioned that in order to have a Concept with a Kicker, you need to develop it with the three other corner pillars, and so these questions are meant to have you start thinking holistically.

So many novels lack a Concept with a Kicker. Of the hundreds of manuscripts I've critiqued, I've seen very few with a strong concept accompanied by a kicker. Many are just same old, same old plots with stereotypical characters and predictable story lines. Nothing *truly compelling* happens in the story. Sure, there may be a scene or two here or there that has a great twist. But as we've seen, a singular twist does not constitute a kicker.

So spend some time thinking about your core concept for your novel. I highly suggest you brainstorm on a piece of paper with a pen or some markers—that's a great way to work on your four pillars (the last chapters of this book share ways to brainstorm your ideas). Start with your basic *idea*. Then work on coming up with a kicker. Answer these questions by thinking up different plot elements that could take your ordinary idea and turn it into a terrific one.

Now that we've covered the first pillar of novel construction, you get your first inspection checklist. These twelve sets of questions are meant to get you to think deeply about the pillars you are constructing and to help sharpen your focus so your novel will be strong. If you can answer them to your satisfaction, you're on your way to building a great novel!

You can download all these checklists as PDFs and print them out to work on. Photocopy the checklist or type this link into your Internet browser: http://bit.ly/16gHs6c.

The PDF that you print out has space for you to write in your answers, so be sure to download and print out copies to keep in your folder.

Inspection Checklist #1
Concept with a Kicker

Question #1:

What is your great idea for a novel? What is the kicker that twists an ordinary idea into something unique, original, and compelling? Try to explain in one clear sentence.

Question #2:

In what ways is your kicker tied in with your protagonist's core need? Greatest fear? Deepest desire? How does his/her goal embody the concept?

Question #3:

What one element or focus makes you excited about your concept? Why will it also excite readers? Can you make it into something controversial?

Question #4:

Picture a movie poster for your novel. What one key scene is pictured on it that embodies your concept and kicker? Describe it.

Question #5:

What is the main gut response/emotional reaction you want your concept to evoke? Explain. Think of ways to tweak your concept so the reaction will be stronger.

Question #6:

What possibilities does the kicker add to your concept in the way of higher stakes and deeper conflict?

Question #7:

What themes, issues, or volatile topics does your kicker involve? Think of at least three and write ways you can add them to the story line.

Question #8:

What iconic scene can you write in your novel that will showcase the essence of your concept and kicker? How can you make it even bigger, more intense?

Question #9:

State your concept with your kicker in one sentence. How can you add in the central conflict and stakes? Can you tweak your kicker so the stakes are even higher?

Question #10:

What happens (or will happen) in the climax of the novel that will show why your concept and kicker are unique and compelling?

Question #11:

What key way will your protagonist change by the end of the novel that ties in specifically with your concept and kicker?

Question #12:

Write down your novel's premise or basic plot idea. Ignoring the kicker you came up with, what three other, different kickers can you think of? Is one better than your initial idea? If so, use it instead.

Pillar #2: Protagonist with a Goal

Chapter 5: A Compelling Novel Centers on the Protagonist's Goal

Do you want to write a compelling story? Think of the word *compel*. *Merriam-Webster's Collegiate Dictionary* has a great definition: "to drive or urge forcefully; to cause to do or occur by overwhelming pressure."

Have you ever read a novel that drove you forcefully to turn page after page? That caused you, by overwhelming pressure, to neglect your chores, your dinner, your kids, in order to get to that last page to see how the book ended? If that's the kind of novel you want to build, then you need to be sure all the elements of your story work together for one main purpose.

You Gotta Have a Goal

What purpose? To follow your protagonist as he strives to reach a goal. Huh? Does that sound too pat to you? I imagine it does, to many writers—especially beginners. Of course, this is just my opinion, and you're welcome to disagree with me (although plenty of writing instructors would be nodding enthusiastically), but the key to a compelling novel is constructing a story in which the hero or heroine is chasing after a goal.

I discussed in the prior chapters the need to focus on the four essential corner pillars first before "building" the rest of your novel—Concept with a Kicker, Protagonist with a Goal, Conflict with High

36

Stakes, and Theme with a Heart. Now that you've got Concept with a Kicker under your belt, we're going to delve into the important aspects of creating a compelling protagonist and how this goal of his or hers is the linchpin for the four corner pillars.

If you don't know what a linchpin is, it's a pin that holds all the parts of a machine or structure together. Without it, whatever you are building will fall apart, collapse. If you write a novel without a protagonist *who is after a goal*, your novel will fall flat. Yes, I will be so bold as to say that is the absolute truth.

Too many novels I critique lack this pillar. Sure, they have a protagonist (usually), but rarely does she have a clear, compelling goal in the story. I'm surprised at how many novels are written that have the main character essentially wandering aimlessly through the pages, without any clear direction, passion, core need, or objective. In other words: no goal.

Well, What Kind of Goal?

What kind of goal does the protagonist need to have in a novel? First off, it has to be a visible one. Something substantial, not esoteric or emotional or spiritual. Yep. That's the first requirement. Screenwriting consultant Michael Hauge really nails this in his workshops and best-selling book *Writing Screenplays That Sell*. Your goal for your main character can't be nebulous, such as "she wants to find love in the end." She needs a very specific goal readers can picture. You should be able to describe your hero's goal to someone in a way that they can see it played out in their mind as if on the silver screen. Why is this important?

Because your novel is a specific story about specific characters needing and wanting something specific. There is no novel without characters. And if the characters don't have any goals, then what is the point to your story? Characters have to have deep core needs, desires, secret fears, impossible dreams. These are the factors that drive the story, like fuel for an engine.

Hauge claims there are only five basic types of goals a protagonist can pursue, and that every strong story uses one of these:

- The need to win (competition, the love of another)
- The need to stop (someone, something bad from happening)

- The need to escape
- The need to deliver (a message, one's self, an item)
- The need to retrieve—(a magic ring, a hidden or lost treasure, a lost love)

This may seem so simplistic that it might be hard to believe. And maybe you think it doesn't even need to be discussed, since it's so obvious. But the protagonist's goal is often glaringly missing from many manuscripts written by aspiring authors.

A Great Novel Is Not Just a String of Events

Without that goal set up near the beginning of the book and which the protagonist strives for until the end, all you have is a string of events. Scenes one after the other in which stuff happens—sometimes interesting, sometimes boring. But if there is no goal established near the outset for the hero, then these scenes serve no purpose and have no point. They lack power and fail to stir up interest. In short, they are not compelling, and are often confusing and unfocused. Readers scratch their heads and wonder, "What is this book about? I don't get it." And that leads to "Why am I even bothering to read this novel?" That's a question writers don't want their readers asking.

Does there really have to be a *point* to a novel?

Yes. If you can't think of "the point" of your novel, just what are you writing about? Oh, yeah. You have an idea. A cool *idea*. Well, what have you learned about ideas in these last chapters? Ideas are a dime a dozen. Ideas do not a great novel make. I think I need some T-shirts made up with these slogans. We writers should drill these truths into our minds.

Let me just say this: If you have a great idea for a novel, and have come up with a compelling Concept with a Kicker, and it *doesn't* include a protagonist with a visible goal, I would sure like to hear about it! I have yet to ever read, in my entire life, a great novel that did not have a protagonist pursuing a goal. Maybe with a literary masterpiece that goal is subtle and not so visible. But I will venture to say it's there.

Ask yourself about your favorite novel or two: What did the hero or heroine of the story want? What was she striving after? Did the climax and ending of the book show her either reaching her goal or failing to reach it? More than likely.

Constructing the Two Goals for the Protagonist in Your Novel

So now you understand that a protagonist must have a visible goal, and that goal needs to be brought out very early in your novel. Usually this is at about the 25 percent mark, but the factors leading to your protagonist fixating on that goal starts sooner. Preferably in the first scene. Why is this so important?

Because you want the reader to "get" what your book—and your main character—is about. Without a clearly defined goal for your protagonist, your reader won't know what the premise is. As I mentioned, the protagonist's goal is the linchpin that connects every element together. Setting up the goal establishes the finish line for your story.

Think about most of the popular movies you've seen. The story opens showing a character in his ordinary world. Something happens to upend it, and a goal is born. Or the movie starts with a character already pursuing a goal, but then something happens and makes it impossible to reach that goal or veers the character in a new direction, pursuing a different goal.

Few authors understand there are really two goals for a protagonist. With every visible goal a character has (and yes, all your main and secondary characters need visible goals), there needs to be an emotional/spiritual goal. This has much to do with your character arc and how each character will change and be changed by the end of the book.

As the protagonist strives to reach her visible goal and faces numerous challenges, obstacles, and choices, the experience changes her. Her goal is tied up with a core need, a passion, a dream. It is something she must get, have, stop, or reach. Her emotional nature and spirituality are tied to that goal.

Is your novel about a man whose child has been kidnapped and now he must go save him? Is your novel about a woman who is greatly opposed to abortion but whose daughter will die if she doesn't abort her baby? Is your novel about a man whose biggest dream is to make it to the top of Everest? Whatever the visible goal is, there is emotional need connected to it (or there'd better be).

That core need or inner motivation drives the character toward his goal, which he may or may not reach at the climax of the book (your choice). But the key to this corner pillar is in establishing and building the visible and spiritual goals throughout the book, where they are both resolved at the same time in the same scene at the climax. That will take some planning and some careful plate spinning.

The Goal Ties In with Theme, Concept, and Conflict

Well, how do you come up with these goals for your protagonist? The first step is to get a clear handle on your concept and kicker. Once you come up with your concept, explore the ways your main character can be the vehicle to showcasing that concept. His goal needs to be centered on that concept, and the themes that are brought out tie in with his core emotional and spiritual needs.

The father seeking to rescue his kidnapped daughter is compelled by fierce love, among many other emotions. The themes that arise from this concept may have to do with self-sacrifice, loyalty, not allowing fear to rule, good wins out—whatever you choose your take-home message to be. If you want to write a story about the death penalty, and you want to show it's wrong, for example, you would create a protagonist with a visible goal that showcases your theme—he might be vehemently opposed to capital punishment (or start with the opposite view, but events cause him to change his belief). Many movies have explored this theme by showing how a person was put to death for a crime he didn't commit. The protagonist may have been the man's attorney, sister, child, or friend.

Goals are tied in with themes. Protagonists need a visible goal that will explore those themes. They need a spiritual/emotional goal that will bring passion and tension to the story. And then conflict and opposition must be positioned to stand in the way of the protagonist reaching his goal (which we'll get into in future chapters). In some ways this is very simple and straightforward. In other ways, it's like trying to keep twenty plates spinning in the air. But with practice and knowledge of the way these plates spin and balance, it can be done—and in a way that looks effortless and easy.

Rather than give you four separate sections on each of these corner pillars, I'm trying to get you to see they work in sync together. You can't just have one; you need all four. They look like four individual pillars that stand alone. But together they bear all the weight

of your story—jointly and in perfect position. If you take one pillar out
or weaken one, it will seriously compromise the integrity of the
structure.

What's in a Character Arc?

We've all heard about character arcs, but I don't see much written
about how you determine just what that arc is. Writers are told
characters have to grow and change, perhaps learn some important life
lesson by the end of the novel. Or maybe not.

There are plenty of novels that don't show much of a character
arc. Rather, the focus of the book is the plot. Genres like thrillers and
romance sometimes are all about plot, with the characters there to
serve the plot, rather than the other way around. Some readers don't
care about character growth or change. And that's fine. Readers read
for many different reasons. There are some books I've thoroughly
enjoyed reading that are hilarious rides or tense suspense, and the
protagonist doesn't "grow" or "learn anything" by the end of the
novel. Part of that is genre; part is the author's choice.

But if that's the case, then the burden of the novel rests on the
plot (and on the engaging writing style), and a writer tackling such a
story will need to be sure to have that clear visible goal for the
protagonist. And that goal should be tying in with the theme and
featuring some very solid conflict (the third and fourth corner pillars)
or the story might have some substantial fatal flaws.

You Still Have to Have a Goal

With or without a strong character arc, know that you still must
have a protagonist with a clear goal. A thriller in which a character is
being chased and is running for his life (such as *The Bourne Identity* and
other thrillers—which I enjoy immensely) may seem like a protagonist
without a goal. But, to the contrary, Jason Bourne and the like have
very clear goals. The goal may be to get through/out/somewhere alive.
And Jason Bourne not only needs to find a place of safety, he also
needs to find out who he really is, which is the kicker to the basic
chase-'em concept. Thrillers that appear to have no real protagonist
goal often have a very strong and obvious one.

So can you create any ol' protagonist? Sure you can—but that
doesn't mean readers will want to read your book. I'm surprised at how

many manuscripts I edit and critique that have either no defined protagonist or one I really don't like. Is it important that readers like your protagonist? If you're not sure of the answer, read on.

Chapter 6: Crafting Empathetic Protagonists

Oftentimes beginning writers have a confused notion about the character arc, thinking that if they open a novel with a really dislikable character who changes by the end of the book into a really likeable guy, that's the ticket. Sorry to say, but it's not.

I wholly believe writers must create a likeable protagonist. Or if not quite likeable, he needs to be empathetic. And there are lots of ways to accomplish this. But don't take too long in the process.

Don't make readers wait to like your protagonist! Why? Because they want to get engaged and start caring for that protagonist *right away*. Did I say "right away"? I did. Meaning, within the first few pages. Preferably on the first page. Try the first paragraph (of the scene in which you introduce your protagonist. It may not be your first scene in the book).

Sheesh, is that really so important? The closer you can get to the first paragraph in hooking your reader's interest in your protagonist, the better. Not a whole lot of readers are going to patiently wait for an author to show something compelling about him. How long are they willing to wait?

I'll wait quite a while, if it's a book by an author I love. I trust (and hope) they will bring me to that place of contentment quickly. But if not, I'll give them a few pages, maybe even a chapter or two. And then I'll give up. But I won't give that much leeway to an author I'm unfamiliar with.

If readers are reading your book and they are not faithful fans, don't expect them to stick around waiting to like your protagonist. Not in this instant-gratification fast-food age. People today want their web pages to load in a matter of seconds, their food to be served in record time, and slow cars to pull over so they can speed by to their destination. Maybe some evocative writing and an unusual setting might buy a few pages of a reader's attention. But not too many pages.

Don't Risk Losing Your Readers

I'm sure there are moans of disagreement out there. However, why risk losing your readers if you don't have to? You don't have to sacrifice your integrity or writing style to accomplish this feat of presenting an appealing protagonist. And there are many ways to make a character appealing. But the best way is to show vulnerability.

Start your novel with a scene in which your character's passion, core need, and deepest fear come into play. These key elements show that a character is human, like you and me. Passion, need, and fear show not only vulnerability but humanity. And what bonds reader to character the fastest is a sense of sympathy. When you create a *sympathetic* character, that's what will hook your reader and make her want to know more.

If you have this as your primary goal for your first scene—to make the reader really like and/or care for your main character—you may have to rethink the starting point for your book. Too often novels start in the wrong place. And usually in places that don't "showcase" well this vulnerability and humanity that are needed.

This is why many literary agents frequently tell writers they are starting their novel in the wrong place. Usually those novels don't really get underway until chapter 3 or 4—when the protagonist starts doing something that shows what an interesting, empathetic, vulnerable, and conflicted person she is. But that's too late.

That Glimpse of Greatness

Let's first take a look at the common type of classic "hero." You want the reader to see something about your protagonist that draws her in, that makes her care what happens to that character.

Literary agent Donald Maass, in his books and workshops, teaches that writers should show a "glimpse of greatness" in the first few paragraphs. I love that phrase. We've been taught that characters should be "larger than life," but I think sometimes that expression confuses. We don't want every character in our novel to be flamboyant or obnoxious or a daredevil. But those types come to mind with a phrase like "larger than life." And besides—how can you get "larger" than life? To me, that implies unbelievability.

Think—what makes a character great? Most writers know they need to portray "an everyday man" or "ordinary people." We want our readers to relate to our protagonist, right? She should be an average Jane, facing the things we ordinary people face, right? Well, yes and no. Yes, it's important to have readers relate to our characters. We need them to quickly care about the protagonist, find her sympathetic. There are lots of great ways to do that, which we'll look at in a moment. The key is in showing the protagonist's humanity, vulnerability, sensitivity, and that glimpse of greatness. All those things are helpful.

But ordinary people are boring. I've critiqued hundreds of novels filled with very boring, average people, and I'm sad to say that I try to care for them, but I simply don't. Readers usually look for any excuse to care for your protagonist. They want to care. Writers, though, shouldn't make this hard for their readers. They should be mindful of wooing the reader right away, getting them attached, bonded, and concerned for the protagonist as fast as possible.

How to Create a Compelling Protagonist

So what can you do to ensure this will happen? Here are some things that make a character empathetic:

- *Put him in trouble.* Readers commiserate with characters facing problems, and especially ones they can relate to.

- *Give him some talent, skill, or admirable ability.* We like characters who excel at something.

- *Make him the victim of some unfortunate circumstance.* As with trouble, readers have compassion for a character who has had to suffer unjustly or due to some tragedy.

- *Make him funny.* We enjoy characters who have a sense of humor, and who might even be self-deprecating or don't take themselves too seriously.

- *Make him kind, noble, generous, gracious.* In other words, give some glimpse that he is a good person with a kind heart.

45

- *Show a glimpse of greatness.* This ties in with the item above. Whether your character is a heroic type, an ordinary Joe or Jane, or a dark brooding negative protagonist, showing some potential to be better, great, or want to change is empathetic.

- *Make him passionate about something.* This is the key to your story as well. For, your protagonist has to pursue a goal, and if he really doesn't care all that much about reaching that goal, readers won't care either.

Spend some time thinking, then, of ways you can show one or more of these qualities in your protagonist—and not just in the first scene in which he appears in your novel. Part of developing that character arc requires you show him grow, change, and learn from the trials and challenges he has to face as he goes after his goal.

What If Your Hero Isn't a Great Guy?

But what if you have a protagonist who is abrasive, antisocial, difficult, struggling, or just plain unlikable? Just how in the world can you get a reader to like such a guy? And yes, it's fine to have a really awful, unpleasant protagonist.

Wait! Didn't I just spend pages emphasizing how important it is to have a protagonist readers will like? How in the world can they bond with and care for someone who is downright unpleasant?

Protagonists like this are called "negative" protagonists or "dark heroes." This type of main character is very popular these days, especially in paranormal and YA genres. You might see a vampire or a depressed teen introduced as the hero of a story. Dark protagonists have been around for a long time. Just think about a movie like the classic *On the Waterfront*, which features a main character who is negative and unhappy. So what's a writer to do to get the reader to like such a loser?

Just be sure that somewhere in the introductory pages in which your protagonist is miserable or unpleasant you show a glimmer of potential. What kind of potential?

Think vulnerability. He may be a vampire or a serial killer, but if he's going to be the protagonist, he has to give some indication that he is not happy with himself, his life, his world. Here you make a promise to the reader that he is going to change, and will be likeable or at least fascinatingly empathetic by the end of the book. How likeable and in what way is up to you. Even a dark protagonist can embody any or all of the characteristics I listed on the previous pages.

The Really Dark Protagonist

The novel *Perfume: The Story of a Murderer* (German author Patrick Suskind) is an intriguing tale about a man in 1738 who was born on the filthy streets of Paris and who has an uncanny sense of smell. Talk about a Concept with a Kicker. This strange character can distinguish scents in a way no human can. He is an evil, possessed man who wants to control the world by creating a perfume drawn from the bodies of beautiful young women, whom he murders to extract their "essence."

Needless to say, this protagonist is despicable, yet he is compelling and intriguing, and his early life calls for the reader to feel some compassion—even starting with his birth, when he is tossed onto a filthy pile of fish, presumed dead. It's a dark story, and not one meant to make readers fall in love with this character. Just as readers don't usually like the abrasive, egotistic, condescending Sherlock Holmes, they are nevertheless gripped by this character's story and personality.

Perfume has a terrific plot, great Conflict with High Stakes (as the protagonist commits one murder after another and finally gets caught), and intriguing themes that deal with the prejudices and fears of those who are different, as well as the consequences of murder, of striving to control others, of taking human life without compunction. We see glimpses of this character's humanity—not his desire to change or become a better person—and perhaps feel some pity for him. He is amazingly gifted, and, as mentioned earlier, that can make a character likeable, because he excels at something (however disagreeable).

You can't get much darker for a protagonist. Was it the author's goal to get readers to actually like him? Surely not. But he definitely created a compelling protagonist that readers wanted to follow. With such a terrific and unusual plot and gorgeous writing, the story hooks and holds the reader all the way through. The ending drives home the message that this is more a fable or allegory than a depiction of true life, and that "fairy tale" quality to the story also provides a bit of exception to the general rule of needing a likeable protagonist. Which makes me think of the movie *Maleficent* and the book *Wicked*. Each features a character traditionally thought of as wholly evil and yet showcases the kicker by presenting these protagonists empathetically.

It's not easy to successfully write a story with a dark, despicable "hero," and that's why most novels don't have them. This type of "hero" is a challenge to write—because all the way through the book you have to be mindful of getting the reader to like him or care about him more and more, even while he might be engaged in horrible or pathetic actions. Yet, a dark hero can be a terrific one—because of the way he grows and changes by the end of the novel.

Dark Heroes Are Not Antagonists

Don't confuse the dark hero with an antagonist. A great antagonist might also change by the end of the book, maybe even feel a twinge of remorse. But a novel is not about the antagonist. The antagonist is placed in the story to support the protagonist (and I don't mean literally or emotionally—I mean structurally). The antagonist acts as an obstacle to the "hero" in reaching his goal. He at times might even be an ally for a time. And the antagonist might not be "dark" or negative at all. (We'll take a closer look at secondary characters and their important roles later in this book when we cover that pillar.)

Sympathy and Resonance

So think instead about creating compelling characters. Remember the definition of *compelling* I gave earlier? It means "to drive or urge forcefully; to cause to do or occur by overwhelming pressure." We want our characters, and particularly our protagonist, to drive readers to keep reading about them. They should be intriguing, unique, perhaps colorful. But mostly, they need to be facing universal issues, struggling with the same kinds of things we ordinary people struggle with.

That's what comes into play when we talk about *sympathetic* characters. The word *sympathy* has this as one of its meanings: "inclination to think or feel alike; emotional or intellectual accord." *Accord* means agreement, harmony. We should be in accord with the protagonist, nodding in agreement, feeling we can relate. Their issues and struggles resonate with ones we've been through.

Resonance is a great word. Something resonates when it's vibrated, stimulated by some outside force. A character resonates with us when outside circumstances cause the character to react and behave in a way that also "vibrates" us in the same way. Another cool definition of *resonance* has to do with two moons in synchronous gravitational relationship as they orbit a planet. I picture myself, the reader, orbiting around the plot and its problems along with the protagonist. We are taken on a journey with him, through his trials and difficulties. We are *compelled* to come along for the ride.

I hope this rather eclectic look at the role of a protagonist has given you some ideas. Whether you feature a classic heroic-type character or a dark protagonist, your goal is to make him compelling. Show that glimpse of greatness in the opening paragraphs. It doesn't have to be a giant "save the cat" moment. A glimpse is a peek, a hint. Oftentimes that's all you need to start your reader caring. And keep this in mind: you don't want to portray a perfect hero. Give that hero some flaws. Make him human so readers can relate. *Resonate*.

So now you know your protagonist needs goals, implying he cares or is passionate about something. And he needs to be sympathetic, vulnerable, and compelling. Is that all? Of course not, but that's what's most essential.

Hey, What about the Goal?

Good question. The character's goal, of course, is what he's all about. It ties in with his core need, passion, dreams, and hopes. As we examined when going over the first corner pillar—Concept with a Kicker—the protagonist's goal is intrinsically tied in with your concept. The Conflict with High Stakes grows out of this character's need and passion. His inner conflict and motivation are what drive him to his goal and make him willing to face huge obstacles with high stakes or consequences. This is basic story structure, time-tested and sturdy, and which makes strong pillars of support for any story in any genre.

You can't just have a really likeable, cool character in your novel—even if he's fascinating, vulnerable, quirky with a larger-than life personality—just going through his life aimlessly. He needs that meaningful goal.

Meaningful for whom? Why, for your character, of course. Done right, you could get readers to root for a character who collects worms or whose goal is to win a cake-baking contest at her church. Seriously? Yes. How can that be done? How can you get readers riveted to a novel about a character with such lame goals as those?

It's all about one word—a word I tend to point out to my editing clients time and again.

Passion

If your protagonist does not have a goal he is passionate about, then it's going to be hard to get your reader to care. There, I said it. I know some of you will disagree with me, but this is the fatal flaw I see time and again. Sure, these novels have a nice protagonist. Maybe a really neat one who is quite unique and engaging. And maybe even sometimes that character will have a goal she is going after . . . sort of.

What I see is a kind of nebulous wandering about with some bit of intention and wanting something that pops up here and there, but nothing focused. From time to time the protagonist may desire something, depending on the scene—which makes the novel seem like a string of scenes, without much purpose or point to the book—a flaw I mentioned earlier in this book. This is so endemic to novels, I can't overemphasize the importance of passion.

A protagonist needs a clearly identifiable goal. Whenever that character gets going after her goal (whether from page one or after some initial disturbance that pushes her through that first "door of no return"), she needs to go after it with passion. It's a simple word, really. Here's how *Merriam-Webster's* defines *passion*: "intense, driving, or overmastering [dominant] feeling or conviction."

Think of the great movies and books you love. Think of the characters in those stories you love. Mel Gibson in *Ransom* (or *Lethal Weapon, The Conspiracy Theory, The Patriot*); Liam Neeson in *Taken*; just about every character in *Lonesome Dove, Legends of the Fall, Downton Abbey*. We've all got our favorites. What makes a great character great?

Passion. Passion with a goal. In a TV series, that "goal" may change from episode to episode, but the passion remains the same. And that passion is all tied up with theme, for passionate people believe in things, and those things are the "themes" of their lives. Even a couch-potato jerk can be passionate with a goal. He may live for the San Francisco Giants and won't touch a pizza unless it's pepperoni and made by the local pizzeria ten miles away. He may only be a secondary character, but he's going to be memorable and compelling if he's passionate about something.

All your characters can be passionate, and all should have goals. Your antagonist, if you have one, will be passionate about stopping your protagonist from reaching his goal. That's *his* goal.

A Reason for the Passion

So spend some time with your protagonist (and eventually all your main characters in your story). Ask him what he's passionate about and why. And be sure to give him good reasons. Passion without reason is like picking characters based on some personality profile charts at random. You're telling a specific story for a specific reason. I hope it's because *you* are passionate about the story you are telling.

To show that passion you have for your story, you populate your novel with characters who feel passionately one way or another about your theme. And when your protagonist is passionate about these thematic elements, you will show him reaching for a goal that will matter—not just to him but to the reader. Why will the reader come to care about that goal? Because you've made him care about your character. It's that simple.

If your character really wants to win that cake-baking contest, and she is passionate for a good reason, and the themes in your book are big (she could want the prize money to save an orphanage, for example), you could have a strong key corner pillar for your novel. Making a cake just to win a blue ribbon will not cut it. Making a cake to save a child's life or to make a dying mother's wish come true will.

It's all about the passion directed toward a meaningful goal.

I hope this has given you something to think deeply about. Don't let the lack of passion in your story be the fatal flaw that causes structural failure. Give your protagonist a goal—an important goal he's passionate about and for good reason. Then see how this takes your story to a higher level.

Checklist time! Photocopy the checklist or type this link into your Internet browser: http://bit.ly/1soYpzN. Be sure to go over all the questions and answer them thoughtfully. If there are some questions you aren't sure of, that should tell you what you need to work on. Some questions may require you to wait until we've gone over all four corner pillars, since you should be engineering your story so that these four corner posts are tightly bolted together. Happy building!

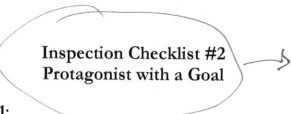

Inspection Checklist #2
Protagonist with a Goal

Question #1:

What is your protagonist's clear, visible goal for the book? How will you hint at that in the first ten pages of your novel?

Question #2:

What does your protagonist want more than anything else (core need)? What is she willing to do to get it? What can make it more dangerous, more impossible to reach?

Question #3:

What spiritual/emotional goal have you set up for your protagonist in the beginning of the book? How will she reach that goal by the end (or fail to)?

Question #4:

Why and how is the protagonist's goal crucial to the overall story? How does it tie in with your concept and kicker?

Question #5:

How does the protagonist's goal reveal the theme of the novel? Explain. What take-home message/emotional response do you want your readers to have after the goal is reached at the end?

Question #6:

How will reaching this goal change your protagonist? How can you make the change much bigger and affect more characters?

Question #7:

What is the biggest obstacle preventing your protagonist from reaching her goal? How can you make it much worse? How can it push her into despair and hopelessness before the climax?

Question #8:

In what ways is your protagonist unique and fascinating, and yet very much like anyone else? What great flaw does he have that will hinder his reaching his goal?

Question #9:

What deep secret is your protagonist keeping, and how will this secret interfere or sabotage him as he strives toward the goal?

Question #10:

What are your protagonist's greatest strengths and weaknesses? What will readers love and hate about her? Can you find a way for her weakness to become her strength?

Question #11:

How will you show something vulnerable, heroic, and/or intriguing about your protagonist in the first scene? Show her gift and handicap.

Question #12:

What very important lesson does your character learn by the end of the book that changes her view of herself and the world and that ties in with your core concept? Write this in one sentence.

Pillar #3: Conflict with High Stakes

Chapter 7: Creating Conflict with a Purpose

Conflict. No one likes conflict. Except, of course, readers of fiction. And, one hopes, writers of fiction. Why do I say "one hopes"? Because I'm surprised by how many manuscripts I edit and critique that have very little to no conflict in the story. And conflict is crucial. Conflict is story.

I might even be so bold as to say that if you don't have a strong element of conflict inherent in your novel, you don't have a novel worth reading (or writing). And this is why conflict is one of the four essential corner pillars in constructing a novel.

We've looked at the first two corner support pillars of novel construction—Concept with a Kicker and Protagonist with a Goal—and now we'll dive into the next corner pillar: Conflict with High Stakes.

But this pillar isn't constructed of just any ol' conflict. Sure, you want to have all kinds of conflict going on in your novel, and we'll be talking about that as we go along. But what needs to be pointed out first, before going any further, is that conflict has to have *consequences*.

Layers of Conflict

Conflict and stakes need to go hand in hand. What point is there in showing characters arguing, for example, if there is nothing at stake? Does it serve the "interests" of the plot to have a husband and wife arguing over what restaurant they will go to for dinner? Without something at stake, something of "value" on the line for those characters, the answer is no. Conflict without purpose (which I'm going to pair with "stakes") only takes up valuable real estate in your novel without accomplishing anything of importance. Throw that scene out. Or rewrite it so the conflict serves a purpose.

Without getting too off track here, note that there are layers of conflict in life—of varying degrees of intensity and consequences—and so our novels should have them as well. So, yes, there can be places for small conflicts that accomplish small essential things in your story. Not all conflict has to be huge.

One Primary Element of Conflict

But amid all the various conflicts your characters will face between the beginning and end of your novel, there should be some *central* conflict that poses *the* main opposition or obstacle for your protagonist. Obstacle to what? By now you should know that answer—the goal your protagonist is trying to reach.

Put simply, the Conflict with High Stakes is intrinsically tied in with your protagonist's efforts to reach her goal for the book. We looked at how that goal needs to be set up early in your novel—a twofold goal made up of a visible plot goal and a "spiritual" goal the character reaches at the climax of the book (and best if both goals are resolved in the same scene).

It's been said there are only a small handful of basic plots, and some tout there are essentially only four—all described by the conflict inherent in the story: man against man, man against nature, man against society, and man against self (and of course you can substitute "woman" for "man" in all of these). In a sci-fi novel like *I, Robot*, you can even have man against machine. But the operative word here is *against*.

Let's take a step back and look at the word *conflict*. One definition *Merriam-Webster's* gives is "the opposition of persons or forces that gives rise to the dramatic action in a drama or fiction." Anything that opposes your protagonist and gives rise to dramatic action is conflict. The tendency for many is to conclude that the central conflict in a novel must be a person, who is presented as the antagonist. And in many novels, that is the case. But conflict doesn't have to mean one individual.

55

Conflict Is All about Your Protagonist's Goal

As implied by these classic plots, conflict can come in other forms. The key, though, is that the conflict must be tailored such that it poses the highest stakes possible in regard to your protagonist attempting to reach his goal for the book. And tied in with this, which we haven't explored yet, is the underlying theme of your story.

We're going to look hard at stakes and what those are. But for now, spend some time thinking about your story. Have you determined what the central conflict element is in your novel? Once you know what your themes are (why you are writing this novel and what "take-home message" you want to give your readers) and what visible goal your protagonist is after, be sure the central conflict inherent in your story creates the greatest opposition possible, with the highest consequences.

In your second checklist you were asked some questions about your protagonist and her goal. How can you make things worse for her, even impossible, as she tries to reach her goal? What or who can oppose her that could force her to risk everything she wants and loves? If you tailor your conflict to create the highest stakes possible for your protagonist, you are on the right track to constructing a strong corner pillar in your novel.

The Secret to Crafting High Stakes

Conflict is crucial to having a compelling story, for if our hero has no obstacles as he tries to reach his goal, the story will be bor-ing. What would *The Wizard of Oz* be like if, once Dorothy arrived in the Land of Oz, she had only to take a walk in the park without incident to arrive back in Kansas? Well, there wouldn't be a story, and story is everything.

So I'll assume we're in agreement that we need conflict in our novels. And regardless of what kind of plot you present in your story, conflict should present high stakes for your protagonist.

The Truth about High Stakes

So just what are stakes? Stakes come in two forms. You may or may not have heard the terms "public stakes" and "personal stakes," but those are, in a nutshell, the two types of stakes at play in a story.

Public stakes affect the world at large. They are stakes that affect others besides your character. That might mean global stakes or small-town stakes.

The best stories, in my opinion, are the ones that have both public and personal stakes in spades. And I'll even say the stories in which the *personal* stakes are the highest are the better stories. I'll explain why in a moment.

Stakes are what is at risk for your character. In general, stakes can be for gain or loss. Characters make choices and initiate action as they go after their goal, and every choice and action should have something at stake—something to gain or lose.

You might assume high stakes (big risks, big losses) only come into play in genres like international thrillers or action/adventure, but I disagree. Any story, however small scale and personal, can present huge stakes and huge consequences. How can that be? Because it's all about the character and her goal.

Yes, we're back to that. Am I starting to sound like a broken record (some of you might even be old enough to know what a record is!)? No doubt. If you create a compelling story with a highly sympathetic protagonist who has a goal that means everything to her, then those stakes, for her, are going to be high. If her happiness lies solely in reaching that goal, then anything that prevents her from her heart's desire is going to be . . . well, heartbreaking—and not just for her but for the reader as well.

High Stakes Are Personal

I could name countless books and movies that work on a small personal scale but bring in universal themes (and that is the key) to bear. One that keeps coming to mind as I write this is the exquisite movie *Fly Away Home*. Okay, it's a movie about a bunch of geese. Right? So why is it when I even *start* to think about this film, tears flood my eyes? Why is it when I listen to the beautiful "theme" song of the movie, "10,000 Miles," sung by Mary Chapin Carpenter, I always cry? Because that movie—a simple story about a young girl named Amy, who gets a flock of geese to relocate to a safe new home—breaks my heart and heals it again in one fell swoop. Okay, call me sentimental.

No, it's not about the geese! It could be about ants or crickets or Twinkies—that's the honest truth. The setting, essentially, is not an issue either. This story could have taken place in Taiwan or South Africa. And many beautiful, powerful stories are set in obscure places featuring one unknown individual dealing with what appears to be a tiny little problem or need. But those are the novels and movies that win awards and high acclaim.

"Big" Is a Matter of Perspective

What's my point? That it doesn't really matter how "big" the conflict is in a story. Big, as in visually or publically big or powerful. What is the central Conflict with High Stakes in *Fly Away Home*? Amy's challenge is to get the dumb birds to follow her as she pilots her flying machine so they can be safe from the mean old Fish and Game warden who wants to clip their wings (is that symbolic for a preteen girl or what?). Or something along those lines. There's a little bit of girl vs. nature as well as girl vs. man (society, the system, etc.). So, why does that meager conflict work? Because of the high stakes.

Huh? How are those stakes high?

They are high because of the *personal stakes* in this film. Amy's mother is killed in a car crash at the beginning of the movie, and now Amy has to move from New Zealand to Canada to live with a father who has been absent from her life and who is the last person in the world she wants to be with. She is in heavy emotional pain and can't cope. She has lost everything in her life that has meaning for her and has no hope. But then—enter the eggs.

A bulldozer clearing the land next to her father's home destroys a nesting site for Canada Geese. Amy gathers up the eggs, latching on to them as if a lifeline to life and sanity, and hatches them using a makeshift incubator. The movie is really about Amy's journey out of darkness into light and hope. A journey that opens her heart to her father and to living again. The geese are the vehicle for this. So naturally, anything that opposes her goal of getting those geese to safety threatens her. A lot.

The stakes, should she fail, *to her*, are huge. They become huge to her father too, as he helps her reach her goal, for their relationship is *at stake*. And of course, their combined purpose brings them together and brings healing to Amy. Conflict and stakes don't get any bigger or better than this.

Stakes Tell Just What the Story Is About

I hope you get my point here. Note that in this movie, the themes are very personal and universal. Loss, family, hope, determination. This is why readers can love stories set in foreign (or even fantasy) places that tell about people very different from themselves. So you should be able to see, for example, that the movie *Signs* is not about aliens, and *The Planet of the Apes* is not about apes. The conflict, stakes, and themes reveal very different stories than expected.

The Kite Runner, a huge best seller and terrific novel, is set in Afghanistan, depicting a culture and life utterly unfamiliar to many of us. Yet the themes and motifs in this book *resonate* (there's that word I spoke of earlier) with readers around the world. Amir's story is a classic one of betrayal, shame, and guilt. When Amir witnesses his close friend Hassan brutalized by a gang of young thugs and he fails, out of cowardice, to help, his guilt plagues him and drives him to do terrible things. Hassan is a messianic figure of self-sacrifice and mercy. The story is poignant and powerful, and the novel is rife with inner and outer conflict.

So I hope this is starting to give you some ideas about stakes and how they must be high—to your protagonist. Every bit of conflict— inner, outer, from any source—that threatens the protagonist's effort to reach her goal equates to serious Conflict with High Stakes.

Keep in mind that genre will determine the kind of conflict and stakes, as well as the seriousness of it all. A lighthearted comedy can have high stakes involving high jinks all in good fun. But those stakes will still create tension and interest. Can anyone say *The Birdcage? (La Cage aux Folles)*. I bit my nails off in suspense watching Nathan Lane serve soup. Conflict? High stakes? You betcha.

Chapter 8: Creating Believable High Stakes for Your Characters

Before I jump into the topic of inner and outer conflict, I'm going to share with you what I feel is the biggest pit writers fall into when it comes to setting high stakes. It's something I see in countless novels I critique. And it's a bad thing—because it threatens believability. If you want your readers to believe in your characters, they have to behave believably. Right?

Here's an example of what I often come across. A character in a fantasy novel goes through some magical portal into another world, where he learns he is the deliverer foretold to save this hidden kingdom. He's your average guy and knows nothing about this world. Without hesitation, he not only accepts the truth of this prophecy/claim/appointment (fill in the blank), he immediately is willing to risk everything—life, limb, future, his firstborn—you name it—to assume the mantle of authority and responsibility.

But why the heck does he do that? I don't know, and neither does the writer. Will the reader really believe someone, anyone, would do that? No. Sorry.

Risk Level Has to Match a Character's True Nature

If you order me (or ask, plead, offer your firstborn) to jump headlong into a raging river (let's say one that leads to a thousand-foot-drop waterfall to my death) to save the ballpoint pen you dropped, do you *really* think I will do that? Even if I were your BFF, would I? No. Most people wouldn't. Unless they were nuts.

But maybe a certain kind of person would, and you could create the kind of character who would believably do that. Someone under a spell? Someone who truly believes the fate of the world rests with that pen? Someone with a death wish? The key to believability lies with the character taking or considering the risk and what *she* believes and is passionate about.

Now, would I jump in that river to save your firstborn?

Hmm . . . that's a better scenario, right? I still might not—depending on the kind of person I am. And maybe you wouldn't either, after taking a hard look at the hopelessness of the effort, and considering you have other children who need a parent to raise them. But it's your precious child. And more than one person has died trying to save a friend or family member—even a stranger—in treacherous waters. This just might be a believable scenario.

Heroes Are Expected to Take Risks, But . . .

Why would someone risk his life to save another? That is a great question to ask—not just to delve into topics of faith, humanity, and sacrifice but also to explore in literary structure. That's what heroes are about, right? They make sacrifices, put others first. We expect and want that from the heroes in our stories. But if the risks they take and the sacrifices they make don't *equal* the values they embody and what they are passionate about, they will not be believable.

And so, your characters need to have *believable motivation.*

If you set up a character to be a selfish, insensitive person, she is not going to risk very much for others—unless she gets some personal benefit from it (gets her closer to her goal). Now, let's discount the character arc for now, since maybe your snooty character is going to change and become all nice and good by the end of the book (but you better have believable scenarios that influence that change as well). The key here is to take care that you set up your characters' personalities, histories, nature, passions, beliefs, and core needs such that when they take risks for something (while going after their goal), the reader believes they really would do such a thing.

Think of movies in which a parent has to go after kidnappers to get his child back (*Taken, Ransom*). Is it believable a father would go through what these characters do to get their kids back? Sure. Wouldn't you do the same? Granted, a lot of dramatic license is taken in these stories, to add to the tension and excitement. We do want to be entertained, right? My husband often hears me grumble at the movie theater or while watching a movie on TV when I see a scene in which a character risks everything for something she just wouldn't care that much about. And when I read similar things in novels, I cringe and want to stop reading.

. . . Make Sure the Stakes Fit the Character

Katniss, in *The Hunger Games*, volunteers to die for her sister—when she takes Prim's place as a Tribute in the games. But we believe her action. Why? Because we already know she deeply loves and is protective of Prim and couldn't bear living with herself if she allowed Prim to participate in the deadly games. Even though this choice is made early on in the book, author Collins made sure we knew enough about Katniss and sympathized with her to wholly believe she would do this. And because of the self-sacrificial theme that resonates, our hearts are wrenched when she speaks out to take Prim's place.

So, as you think of ways to establish high stakes for your characters, be sure the stakes and the risks they will take align with their nature, values, and personality. Don't ask me to believe your protagonist is willing to risk all to save the world unless what she has to lose by refusing to do so is unthinkable—to her.

Characters' Passion = Risk They Are Willing to Take

Always keep this in mind: the passion a character has must be equal to the "penalty" he will pay if he doesn't take the risk, and it's commensurate to the value the character places on the thing at risk. If something is precious to your character, he will be willing to risk much to get, save, protect, or retrieve it (visible goal). The more value this object or objective has, the more you can push the stakes higher. And the higher, the better. That way, any conflict introduced that threatens will be big.

Big threats, high stakes, great risks—all make for solid novel structure. So build your corner pillar of Conflict with High Stakes with deliberation and careful attention. It will provide excellent support for your novel.

Introducing Conflict into Your Story

Conflict is crucial in a novel, and it doesn't have to come from just one main source or one clearly defined antagonist. We explored the topic of stakes and looked at how high stakes are measured by the value the protagonist puts on the thing at stake. (And this applies to all other characters in your book as well.) In essence, the stakes are high if what is being risked is highly valued. These are personal stakes.

Although I haven't elaborated on "public" stakes (what is at risk for others in your novel or "the world at large"), just keep in mind that any and all stakes have to concern your hero. If there are going to be large consequences because of his choices—ones that affect others on a small interpersonal level, community level, or even global level—he has to care about those repercussions—because the book is essentially about him, his choices, and his goal. Depending on the genre, stakes and their consequences will vary. But a great novel will have conflict and high stakes at its core.

Introduce the Conflict as soon as Possible

Although it's best if the central conflict element in your story is introduced as quickly as possible, it may not work with your plot to do so from the get-go. Certainly, the sooner the reader can be introduced to the protagonist's goal for the book, the better. And when that goal is presented, that's the time to bring in the obstacles that are in her way (some you can set up right at the start of your novel). And compound them as much and as soon as possible.

Runaway best-seller *The Art of Racing in the Rain* (one of my all-time favorite books) is told from Enzo's point of view. Enzo is an old dog, and he tells the story of his owner, Denny, who marries and has a baby with his wife. There is very little conflict, if any, at all for many chapters in the book as we get to know this dog and his family, which is highly entertaining and engaging even without any conflict (and that's a hard thing to pull off—because that tension is lacking). But just when we need some conflict, it comes barreling in.

Denny's young wife gets ill and dies. Then, to his shock, her parents decide they want custody of his beloved daughter. And they will stop at nothing to get her—even go so far as to set him up for a big fall by having him falsely accused of rape. The rest of the book is embroiled in this central conflict of man against his in-laws (is that universal or what?). And it gets worse and worse and more and more hopeless for Denny.

I have to share my favorite moment in the book. At the height of despair (Denny's dark moment of the soul), when he feels so hopeless and beaten that he has decided he must give in (the stakes are too high now for him to go after his goal of custody because he has to think of his daughter's welfare above his own), he reaches for the legal agreement to sign that gives his in-laws custody. Even his friends' urging won't make him change his mind. But then Enzo, who understands exactly what is going on and is not a bit happy, pees all over the papers. Take that! That hilarious, poignant, symbolic gesture is not lost on Denny and is all he needs to rally his resolve to fight for what is most precious to him. This is the turning point that rushes the book to its terrific climax and resolution.

The conflict did not appear right away in the book, but author Garth Stein did not just ignore it or put it off. He didn't just plop it in at a random moment. He carefully set all the pieces in place for it to arrive. Earlier in the book we meet the in-laws and learn something about them before they descend like wolves. We watch Denny fall in love with his wife and see what a great, devoted parent he is. Everything, then, is in perfect place for the introduction of the conflict.

Just as in the movie *The Perfect Storm*. The storm doesn't hit in the opening scene, but we know it's coming. The anticipation of conflict brewing (literally) on the horizon can add tremendous tension to a story. But you have to prepare the stage for its arrival so it feels big.

To Reiterate . . .

Simply stated: conflict is anything that stands in the way of your character reaching her goal. And that can be internal or external. The other primary characters in your novel are going to have goals too, and those should be goals that impact your protagonist and her goal. So, it stands to reason that they too should face conflict.

The more conflict the better. The messier, the better. Conflict should start at one level and keep rising and getting worse. Generally the middle of your novel is the muddle—where you muddle everything to make it harder and harder for your character to reach her goal.

Also simply stated: The conflict will include high stakes if what is risked or threatened is precious to your character. Which is what you want.

I know this is sounding repetitive to you by now, and maybe it just seems too simple. But if you work with this basic framework (think: building construction), you will have that sturdy foundation.

Spend time thinking about the central conflict element in your story and all the different ways it can raise ugly heads to threaten and upend your protagonist. Try to pit as many things against him as you can, and push the stakes so that what he values most is at risk of being lost. If you build your corner pillar in this way, it will support just about any novel you create.

Chapter 9: A Look at Inner and Outer Conflict

Let's take some time to talk about the two faces of conflict: inner and outer. Maybe I don't need to go over outer conflict because it's obvious, right? Anything *outside* your character that hinders him or opposes him is external conflict. And usually this is easier to construct than internal conflict. But there are some things to keep in mind about external conflict.

I mentioned that you should have a central element of conflict in your story, but let me explain this a little further.

It's possible you may have one individual or thing acting in direct opposition to your main character that is his greatest obstacle or challenge. It may be another person, an evil beast or demon, an element of nature (an oncoming tornado or nuclear winter, for example), or a more abstract opponent, such as society or law or "the system." A lawyer trying to take a case to the Supreme Court can be fighting society and the legal system, and so instead of one person opposing him, conflict can come via many people and circumstances. The central conflict might encompass a number of elements, but it will still be "man against society," unless this is a personal battle, such as in the 1970s movie *Kramer vs. Kramer*, which is more "man against man" (or woman).

So, to think in terms of a general, overarching central conflict element in your story, you need to go back to pillar #1: Concept with a Kicker. Your concept needs to be tied in with the central conflict of your story.

Always Ask Questions!

Let's say your novel is about a married woman who desperately wants to have a baby and is willing to risk just about anything (high stakes) to get pregnant and have one. You need to determine just what the primary opposition is going to be for her. What is she willing to risk? What if her husband is sterile? What if she, he, or both do not want to adopt? What choices does she face, and what would the consequences be by acting on them?

If you want this story to have great Conflict with High Stakes, your character might consider getting pregnant in secret, outside her marriage. Enter deception, lying, prevaricating, betrayal. What if she asks her best friend's husband to impregnate her? Think of what a mess that could make—all because she wants a baby more than anything else. Would she kill? You could push her to that point. Plenty of people have killed to hide their affairs (makes me think of the Scott Peterson trial).

Without needing to point this out, we are talking here about a protagonist and her goal. Her core need. These are questions you can ask to help you elevate both private and public stakes:

- What will she do if that core need isn't met?

- How far can you muddle, push, or exacerbate the situation to raise the personal and public stakes?

- How many (more) people can you involve and affect by her choices?

- How many lives can you ruin? (This is where you can come up with the great subplots for your secondary characters.)

- What allies can turn into foes by her choices and actions?

- How can you complicate things so that it (seemingly) becomes impossible for her to reach her goal? What will she do now that will make things even worse for herself and others?

- What core beliefs of hers can be challenged?

- Can you push her to have to choose between two options, both unthinkable (think *Sophie's Choice*)?

Notice how the inner conflicts interweave with the outer ones. Every time your character struggles internally and has to make a hard choice, *it creates consequences of outer conflict.*

Literary agent Donald Maass says, "Inner conflict is an interior war." When your main character has two desires that are mutually exclusive, it's a dilemma. This is not just inner confusion, though. Inner conflict has to present clear issues with clear repercussions. The choices your character makes have to be deliberate, done with knowledge of the stakes, risks, and consequences.

Although we haven't gotten into theme yet, consider this: whatever issues your story is showcasing by the plot, create conflict by having others take views that stand in opposition to your protagonist's. Like plot layers, conflict can be thick or thin. Big and important or small and irritating. The best novels have conflict on many levels, all working cohesively to oppose your character. And as we'll see later when we look at the pillar Plot in a String of Scenes, these forces build to a climax in which protagonist and conflict clash head-on.

Don't Be Nice

Sometimes we writers really like our characters. We may even love them so much we hate to make them uncomfortable or hurt them. Our job as novelists, however, requires that we be a bit heartless. Okay, maybe more than a bit. For how can a hero triumph without conflict and high stakes? How interesting is that novel going to be if there is no obstacle in the way of him getting his heart's desire?

From what I've seen in the hundreds of manuscripts I've worked on, conflict and stakes are way underplayed. Writers are too nice to their protagonists. Conflict is narrow, too small in scope. Asking these types of questions (above) can help push you to create higher stakes, bigger risks, greater possible losses, more collateral damage, and horrible choices. Now that's the recipe for a page-turner.

Think of ways to create lots of internal conflict (hard choices) and external conflict (lots of opposition from every direction), and you'll have a strong corner pillar.

Emphasis on Inner Conflict

As we wrap up our look at this third corner pillar of novel construction, I'd like to make a few other observations about conflict. We looked at inner and outer conflict, and how the best novels have both types of conflict in great measure and in various strengths involving as many characters and situations as possible. Messier is better when it comes to conflict, and we have to resist the tendency to be nice to our hero or heroine.

It's possible to have a strong novel with just inner conflict and little external conflict. You could have a story that follows the classic "man against nature" in which a character is shipwrecked on an island and never sees another soul. Think of the movie *Castaway*, which might have started out as a "man against nature" story. But at some point the protagonist masters nature. He learns to fish and finds a way to survive without too much effort or challenge. Then what's the story really about? Where's the conflict?

In a case like this, the central conflict element of the story just might center on a character trying to keep from losing hope. Or you could be writing a novel about a person in solitary confinement for ten years. If done well, it could be terrifically tense and gripping even if nothing "goes on" outside the character's mind. But these are unique premises that perhaps create a situation in which the external conflict is minimal. By this I mean there is no active person or element acting directly and personally against him. Yes, the circumstances act as an opponent of sorts, something to be mastered or conquered. But it's the arena of the inner conflict that is the focus of such a story.

Most novels really need both inner and outer conflict. In other words, you could have a strong novel with very little external conflict, but a novel with just exterior conflict and *no inner conflict*, in my opinion, will fail.

Why? Because stories are about characters, and characters must change over time or you don't have a story. What causes change in us is inner conflict. Until something you believe or think is challenged, you will not change your views, opinions, attitudes, behavior, or core beliefs. And a character who never changes is boring.

I will also be so bold as to say this: if the inner conflict is *way* bigger than the outer conflict, it will act as an amplifier to the outer conflict and make it much more significant. For example, you could have a suspense thriller with a killer plot that has great twists and tense action (think: James Bond movies). But if you add to the mix a protagonist with huge inner conflict, someone who is fighting with himself, his past, and/or his inner demons, you will have a much stronger and more compelling story.

As I mentioned in an earlier chapter, we want to resonate with the characters in a novel. The best way to create resonance is to show vulnerability. What is one great way to show vulnerability? Make your characters conflicted.

Which brings me to something I've been thinking about while writing about conflict.

Life without Conflict Is Like . . .

Think for a moment what life would look like without conflict. If you could go through every day without any opposition. Without anyone challenging what you feel or believe. Without anything in your way as you put out the effort to reach your goals and accomplish your dreams. No competition, no one to question you or your motives and actions. No conflict.

Sounds great, right? Paradise, heaven, perfection. We say we love conflict in the stories we read because that is what real life is like, but what if real life *wasn't* like that? What would we miss out on?

Hmmm . . . some of you may be shaking your heads and saying, "Miss out on? What the heck?"

The Refining Process of Precious Metals

My pastor gave a talk once on refining silver, since the Bible speaks a bit about faith and how it has to be tested and refined to be of any value. In fact, the Bible likens refined faith to silver and gold, precious metals of high value. He spoke about how when silver is heated to extreme temperatures, the impurities or dross rises to the top of the molten metal so it can be skimmed off. That's how the metal can be purified, improved, made more valuable. Likewise, the trials we go through in life are a crucible that provides a way for us to face the "ugly" dross within us, to get it to the surface so we can skim it off and become better people.

Maybe some would argue that trials, tests—conflict—only aggravate and burden our lives with pain and grief. And that is certainly true. No one in their right mind wants to suffer or struggle with conflict. But thinking along those scriptural lines, we might look at the upside of trials.

Conflict makes us face our flaws and weaknesses. It reveals to us hidden things about ourselves, often painful things (perhaps from past hurts), and often gets to the core of our motivation, showing why we do the things we do. Conflict makes us reconsider our values, ethics, morals, decisions, and attitudes. The higher the stakes we might face in a situation, the more at risk and the more we have to lose, the more we have to look honestly at ourselves and what we want, need, and desire. We cannot grow or change for the better without some of this honest assessment because change on a significant scale has to be deliberate.

Conflict Is Good for Us

If we're honest (and brave), we might just say we need conflict. Conflict is good for us. Conflict is essential to healthy emotional growth. We stand up to opposition when we voice things we believe in or injustices we won't tolerate. Humans have varying opinions. They disagree on issues large and small. Conflict is life. And so, we want the characters in our novels to be real and believable. For them to grow, change, and learn, they need to be thrown into a crucible. They need the fire of conflict to bring that dross to the surface. Whether they will learn from the trials they go through is up to you, the author. But if you don't throw them into the fiery furnace, the reader won't get to see their flaws and weaknesses and desperation rise to the surface.

I like to think that the fire of tribulation also brings out the true essence of character (even if only a glimpse), and that is a valuable consequence as well. If a character can have a moment in your novel in which he sees himself as he truly is—a mirror moment—that is usually a pivotal moment. What he does when he "looks in the mirror" is, again, up to you, the writer. In most great novels, that moment comes right before or at the climax, and it acts as a huge motivational thrust to push the character to make the big final decision/action that brings the story to a conclusion. In other words, the biggest challenge/trial/conflict reveals the biggest truths to the character, forcing him to face the hardest facts about himself.

So I hope this discussion about conflict and stakes has given you a lot to consider as you structure your novel (or restructure it). Conflict, inner and outer, is a key pillar to a great story. And the conflict must have stakes—high stakes—and if possible, public and personal stakes.

Don't be afraid to put your characters in the crucible of fiery trials. It will bring out all the ugly, hidden things that reveal the core of motivation for both your good guys and your bad guys.

And now, you get your third inspection checklist. Photocopy the checklist or type this link into your Internet browser: http://bit.ly/1xbQ5dt. This set of twelve thought-provoking questions will help you examine the Conflict with High Stakes in your novel. If you can answer these questions to your satisfaction, and see that you have the central conflict element clearly defined and the stakes as high and as wide-reaching as possible, you will have a strong support pillar that will not crumble under the weight of your story.

Inspection Checklist #3
Conflict with High Stakes

Question #1:

What is the central (outwardly visible) conflict in your novel? Who or what is preventing your protagonist from reaching her goal?

Question #2:

Just how does this conflict element pose problems for your protagonist? Now, can you make it much bigger, much worse? List some possibilities and their outcomes.

Question #3:

What are the personal stakes at risk due to this conflict in your story? Can you raise the stakes more? How? In what ways?

Question #4:

What are the things your protagonist loves and cherishes the most? Can you set up the conflict so that he stands to lose those as he goes after his goal?

Question #5:

What public stakes are threatened by this central conflict component? Who and what else will be adversely affected if the protagonist fails to reach his goal? Can you make it worse?

Question #6:

What will happen right before the climax of the novel to show the conflict at its peak? How will this push the hero into a dark night of the soul?

Question #7:

How can you make the conflict elements more personal so that it's more painful for your main character? Who can betray her? Fail her?

Question #8:

In what way is your central conflict embodying your theme? How does the conflict force your protagonist to make thematic choices in the novel, with the hardest choice at the climax?

Question #9:

How will the conflict component be resolved or eliminated (or left a threat) at the end of the novel so that it is satisfying and believable to readers?

Question #10:

What strong inner conflict is your protagonist dealing with? Come up with two things she must choose between, both unthinkable. Tell how this showcases your novel's theme.

Question #11:

Can you come up with at least five minor, different conflict components you can add to your plot that exacerbate the central conflict of your novel?

Question #12:

How does your protagonist change by the end of the book due to the central conflict? How do her attitude and actions toward that conflict change, and as a result, how does the conflict itself change?

Pillar #4: Theme with a Heart

Chapter 10: Theme—What's at the Heart of Your Story

So far, we've looked at three of the four corner pillars that are the essential supports for your story, and you've been given your "inspection checklists" so you can test your pillars to see how well they hold up your story. Those first three are Concept with a Kicker, Protagonist with a Goal, and Conflict with High Stakes. We're now going to explore corner pillar #4: Theme with a Heart.

Hey, What about Plot?

Hmm, I already hear some of you saying, "Huh? What about plot? Isn't plot one of the most important pillars—if not *the* most important? How can you support a novel without the plot being the key component of the story?"

Good questions.

I don't consider plot a key corner pillar, and I'll explain why. And this doesn't mean I think plot is unimportant; it certainly is crucial. A great plot is key to a great story. But it's not as important as a compelling concept. Or a protagonist with a clear goal. Or presenting a theme that is at the heart of your story. It's not really a pillar at all.

Let me just say this: tension in a story has little to do with plot. Huh?

Plot Is What Happens—That's All

Plot is all about what *happens*. Plot is "this happens first, then this happens next." And on and on until you get to the end of the book. But without concept behind and driving the plot, all you have is a string of possibly interesting scenes.

Without a protagonist with a compelling goal, a plot, in the end, will fail to "hold up" the "house" you are building. It will be pointless to show a bunch of "exciting" things happening without providing the reader with someone to care about, despise, root for, or worry over.

Stories are about people (at some point, someplace in the story). Or, rather, about *characters*. Maybe your world is populated with animals (*Animal Farm*, for example) or aliens or robots. As I mentioned in an earlier chapter, *The Art of Racing in the Rain* has a dog for the protagonist (first-person narrative). But let me say this—which is the key: Enzo the dog is one of the most *human* characters I've ever read in a novel, and that's why readers love that book. The more truly human your protagonist is, the more readers will relate. That character will *resonate* with them.

Theme is more important than plot in terms of supporting the whole of your story, and that's why it's the fourth corner pillar of novel construction. I called plot a vehicle for your theme. It's also the vehicle to showcase your concept, protagonist's goal, and central conflict. In other words, try to think of plot as functioning differently than the other elements in your story. We will take a look at plot next as one of the pillars in novel construction, but it's the *structuring* of the plot itself that we'll focus on—since this book is all about building a story. It speaks to the framework of your "house" rather than the actual materials.

Theme Is What It's All About

Why am I directing you back to all these points we covered? To make my argument for theme being the necessary fourth pillar. Why theme? Some of you might argue that a lot of novels don't even have a theme—maybe even great novels. But I will be so daring as to challenge those who say such things and claim, "Yes, they do. You just aren't looking hard enough."

Here's what I would say to an author who claims his novel doesn't have a theme at its heart. (Well, if it's a poorly structured novel, it may not. But for argument's sake, let's say it's a great novel.) My first question would be: "What's your novel about?" After the author gives me his answer, which is solely about plot, I would then say, "Now, tell me what your novel is *really* about."

Stop for a moment and think. Underneath all the plot layers of various sizes and colors and tastes lies something fundamental. Something at the heart of a story. Ask yourself, "What's my novel about?" Then ask yourself: "What is my novel *really* about?" without talking about the plot. It may take some digging, but you will arrive at an answer that speaks to theme.

Ask Questions to Get to Your Theme

Think of theme another way. Ask yourself, "*Why* am I writing this novel? What excites me about the idea? What moved me to take this idea and form it into a Concept with a Kicker? Why do I love my protagonist? What excites me about the conflict in my story, and why do all these things *matter to me*?" And my favorite: "Why am I willing to spend months of my life slaving over this story—what is compelling me to such madness?"

Wow, is this a whole lot of psychoanalysis or what? Do writers really need to grill themselves with all these questions, and do they really have to know the answers? Well, of course not. Writers don't have to do anything, if they don't want to. You may want to write a book completely ignoring and unconcerned with theme. You may be all about plot, thank you, and nothing else. That's fine; go there.

But I'm going to be a stickler and say that even if you write a novel with that mind-set, if that novel turns out to be any good, there are going to be some themes supporting it. Maybe small ones, but themes nevertheless.

If you can answer those questions, and also answer "What is my story *really* about?" you will get to the heart of your story—which is your theme.

Just What Is Theme in a Novel, Anyway?

Since theme is what a story is really about once you look beneath the plot, and theme is tied in with the writer's passion and interests, asking those personal questions about why you are writing turns the focus away from the actual story and toward your writer's heart. By

78

exploring why you are so jazzed about telling a certain story, you can mine rich themes and develop them.

Too often writers don't consider theme or even think their novel has one (or more), but I believe every story is about something more than plot. Or if it isn't, it can and should be. Theme is a glue that holds all the novel components together: characters, setting, conflict, plot, and, well, just about everything else. It sticks it all together. It's like yeast in dough that makes your story expand and fill out. No plot, and you have a flat "yeast-less" lump of dough. Okay, enough with the metaphors, right? I'm sure you get my gist.

Breaking Down Theme

So maybe you're wondering if you really know what theme is. I'll try to break it down. Just know, as with high stakes and protagonists' goals and the purpose of your concept, there are varying degrees to theme. Genre plays a part, certainly. Writing style as well. Some books, as I mentioned in a previous chapter, are just fun rides, seemingly without any point other than to entertain. Other books practically drip with theme.

I've read nail-biting suspense that's clearly been written to take the reader on a ride, so that by the end of the book it's like climbing out of your seat on the roller coaster all shaky and nauseated. But you slap your friend on the shoulder and say, "Wow, that was awesome, dude!" Is theme an important structural element in those types of novels? Yes—or I should say, the better suspense novels will have some strong themes. And as you learn more about theme, you'll be able to identify them easier with every book or movie or play you examine.

Theme has two definitions in *Merriam-Webster's Collegiate Dictionary* that come into play here. The first: "a subject or topic of discourse." The second: "a specific and distinctive quality, characteristic, or concern."

This brings me back to my earlier questions. Why did you choose this premise or idea to write about? What compelled you to spend months of your life telling this particular story? What *quality, characteristic, or concern* surrounding your idea grabbed you and why?

Why Is Theme Important?

Why would you want rich themes? To take your story to another level. Themes turn good novels into great ones. Themes take the story you have and make it better, deeper, more meaningful, more resonating, more universal. In other words, theme brings all your novel's elements together in purpose and presents life in a realistic, complex way. Universal themes translate into novels that stand the test of time.

Life and people are not simple. Motivation is never cut-and-dried. Themes force characters (and hopefully readers) to ask questions— about life, themselves, what they believe, how they view others. Theme reflects the heart of life, and hence, the heart of a story.

Draw Your Themes to the Surface of the Story

The great thing is theme doesn't necessarily have to be completely worked out at the start—unlike the other four pillars. Even if you have some general idea of theme, and you've spent time asking yourself (and answering) the questions on your inspection checklist that will help make clear exactly what your themes are and how you can bring them out, you can come back time and again into your scenes to develop the themes.

By going through your first draft with the intention of finding ways to have characters and events showcase your themes, you can add moments or heighten tension around thematic issues. You might change your book's title to reflect or play off of theme. You might bookend your theme by working it into the first and last chapters. Theme is like a flavor you can distribute throughout, which will enhance your story overall.

Themes Are Not Just Topics

Themes are not just topics or subjects, which takes us back to the contrast between idea and concept. You might say your book is about abortion or capital punishment. That is just the topic (idea). Ask: What am I saying about that topic through my characters? Whether you are taking a strong stance or none at all (just want to explore the topic), in order to have a story with a plot, with characters who care about something, you will have theme.

Think about that dictionary definition of *theme*—"a specific concern." The operative word is *concern*. Someone, somewhere in your novel, is concerned about something—something bigger than just what to eat for breakfast or what clothes to wear. It's the job of your characters to embody or showcase your themes, and as we learned in the chapters about your protagonist, *everything* in a novel swings back around to the protagonist's goal. This is what's at the heart of your story and the heart of your theme.

Theme Is Connected to Concept, Protagonist, and Conflict

If your concept involves astronauts on a dangerous mission to Mars, for example, and you are writing action/adventure/suspense, what is your theme(s)? Well, that depends on your other pillars: the concept (premise with that kicker), the protagonist and his goal, and the central conflict highlighting high stakes.

Let's look at the protagonist's objective in the movie *Red Planet* (which is also the collective goal of all the characters)—which is to get to Mars to see if the experiment to grow algae is a success. That may or may not present a viable or engaging theme. With that idea, you might have a purposeless string of scenes as they get to the planet (or not) and face danger or obstacles. In other words, it could have been a lousy movie.

But here's the concept and kicker for that movie: It's 2055. Earth can no longer feed all its inhabitants, so this is a desperate measure to save humanity (great concept and kicker, danger/conflict potential and high stakes, clear goal). By setting up this story with three strong corner pillars, it makes the way for great themes. How so?

Interestingly, there are a lot of themes going on in *Red Planet*, which makes it a rich and fascinating story in addition to the basic action/adventure going on as one thing after another goes wrong and the characters die one by one. The *plot* is exciting and well structured, which is key.

But as I mentioned previously, plot means little if the four main structural components (corner pillars) aren't built to perfection. This movie would just be a string of scenes, albeit interesting ones, just because of the plot. Their emergency landing is met with disaster, provision losses and equipment malfunctions add more danger and devastation, and a high-tech robot goes Terminator on them. However, this movie is much more compelling because of its themes.

What the screenwriters did to make the way for themes galore in this story was to create a cast of characters from different scientific disciplines, each passionate about something that clashes with other characters' passions. When you have characters conflicting because of their worldview, beliefs, morals, and priorities, you have the ingredients for rich themes in your story.

Theme Emerges in Conflict

I proposed early on in this book that "conflict is story." In *Red Planet*, the scientists must struggle to overcome the differences in their personalities, backgrounds, and ideologies for the overall good of the mission. Note that they share a common goal, but each has different passions and beliefs. When their equipment suffers life-threatening damage and the crew must depend on one another for survival on the hostile surface of Mars, their doubts, fears, and questions about God, man's destiny, and the nature of the universe become defining elements in their fates. In this alien environment, they must come face-to-face with their humanity.

Plot *shows* the story; theme *is* the story. Plot is the vehicle for theme. This is a good mantra to repeat as you plot out your novel.

Note, though, that these themes don't crop up in the movie through a mundane string of philosophic discussions. The wonderful moments in which these topics and themes come out take place while the action is ongoing and tense. Sure, great stories (movies, plays, or novels) will have those reflective or introspective moments in which the characters discuss, think, and/or question their views and beliefs. This is crucial because character arc is all about change and growth. But those should be brief moments of reflection positioned between the active scenes.

Theme Is Reflected in Your Characters' Changes

What makes your characters change is intrinsically tied in with your book's theme. If you don't know what your primary theme is, think about the key moments in your book that force your character to change his view on something (which will lead to action). I would go so far as to say this: If you think about your protagonist's key moment of realization that occurs right before or at the climax of your novel, that's where your theme can be found. If you don't have that moment, you don't really have a strong character arc. And that can be a problem.

Chapter 11: Constructing Theme

When I started contemplating what to write about this pillar, I realized I didn't have a whole lot to say. Theme isn't often discussed as a crucial element in a novel, but to me it is one, and is mostly overlooked or taken for granted. Do writers simply assume theme will just show up and needs no introduction? I'm not sure.

When I searched online for articles about theme in novels, I could hardly find a thing. And that disturbed me. I'm all about theme, and even when I get an idea for a new novel and a scenario or concept comes to mind, I instinctively head for the theme. In fact, the theme is my litmus test for whether a novel idea has potential. If it's just a cool idea but I can't connect it to a meaningful theme, out it goes. I usually don't have that problem, though, because themes are the germs of stories for me, so they usually spark the idea.

How to Come Up with Themes

So what are some ways you can come up with themes for your story? Or come up with a story with a great theme? One way, as I mentioned, is to take a look at your characters and see what they are passionate about. But what if they aren't passionate about anything? If that's the case, you haven't worked hard enough with your idea to create a strong Protagonist with a Goal. And for that character to want to strive for a goal, she has to be passionate about something. Find her passion, and you have the germ for the themes.

Have you worked out the central conflict in your story—something that opposes your character? That conflict will present your themes, as those opposing your protagonist have an agenda and core need (passion) and most likely will take some side or view on an issue or behavior or belief that is in opposition to the one your protagonist embraces.

Go back to the questions I posed earlier in this discussion about theme. Ask yourself, "What is my novel about?" Then ask yourself, "What is my novel *really* about?" Roll up your sleeves, and do some digging. There is a lot under the surface of your concept that you can mine for theme.

Another way that helps me find theme is by asking questions. Why, why, why? This speaks to the heart of motivation. With any developing concept you're considering fleshing out into a full novel, ask lots of questions to arrive at themes that excite you.

Everyone's process in going from idea to finished novel is different. I've experimented with many methods, and over the course of writing more than a dozen novels I've come up with the process that works best for me. I am not talking about the way I create outlines or charts or write scenes on index cards (which I do for almost every novel). I'm talking about the creative process of bringing random, chaotic ideas into order. And the way I do this gets me targeting the essentials of the four corner pillars right away—especially theme.

An Example of How I Flesh Out Theme

I'm about to write a dark-comedy novel called *The Menopause Murders*. Okay, I realize I'm taking a huge risk here, because, as you know (since I shared with you the fun definition of high concept earlier), someone is going to steal this idea. I just hope they don't kill me over it. My feeling, though, is no one will write the book *I'm* planning to write. I'm sure they just won't end up with the novel I picture in my head. Because my life experience is unique (and yours isn't the same as mine).

So, here's my concept: A mousy, weak housewife, who is dominated by an irritating, arrogant husband and who suffers two obnoxious, spoiled teenaged children, suddenly gets broadsided with menopause. (Sorry, guys, you really will never be able to write this story—except from the husband's point of view, and that's why I've enlisted a male author friend who has survived menopause to cowrite with me).

I have a great idea for the opening scene, and I have the basic story line: My protagonist goes online (which I did when I got a weird symptom I could not figure out), and learns there are thirty-five—yes thirty-five—symptoms of menopause. After hearing shocking and hilarious stories at my writers' lunch from numerous women who somehow survived menopause (not sure how many of their husbands did), I formulated this idea. My character will get all thirty-five symptoms over a period of time (TBD, but most say menopause averages four years. My condolences to those of you who have suffered longer).

What's my heroine's goal? To get through menopause alive. The kicker? Every time she gets a new symptom, she murders someone (yes, really). By the time she is done with menopause, she's murdered thirty-four people. Wait, I said thirty-five symptoms. Yes, but the last symptom she gets is short-term memory loss, so at that point she will forget she's killed anyone, or wanted to (nice twist at the end).

Okay, I have a great Concept with a Kicker and a Protagonist with a Goal. I'm creating conflict (her husband will be the detective investigating all these murders, her children will hate her new personality, she'll get fired from her job, she'll end up divorced, and on and on). I'm not sure of the climax yet, but I know in the end she'll have reinvented herself, gotten a new man and a new career, and live blissfully happily ever after, completely ignorant of her crimes, with the murders unsolved.

I picture a very funny *Kill Bill*–style tone, but even while coming up with all these things, my main focus was on theme. Why? Because this story could be about a ton of things. It could be just a fun ride (wasn't that the point of *Kill Bill*? I mean, really, do those kinds of movies have themes?).

Theme Comes out of Passion

Remember I spoke about the way to find your themes? You need to explore why you want to write the story you are writing (or planning to), which will require you to give up months of your life to accomplish. Why are you doing this to yourself and your family? Because there is something about the idea that is compelling you.

So here's what compelled me to even start brainstorming this story. 1) the fact that quite a few women I know have cancer (and some have died) after the onset of menopause due to hormone treatments 2) women often feel old, useless, and washed up as a woman when they go through this "change of life," and 3) they often suffer the effects of ageism/discrimination of old age (even if not old).

What compelled me to even think of this as a novel were those things I began to be passionate about. What I cared about. I cared that women were dying of cancer because their doctors gave them drugs without warning them of the danger. I cared that women feel invisible, oppressed, and put down because of their age. I cared that many women are dumped by husbands (some because of those menopause symptoms) who go after much younger women (no, this hasn't happened to me; my husband is a great guy), whereas it's almost impossible for women to dump their husbands for younger men. Theme galore.

Are Message-Heavy Novels Bad?

No, I don't plan on making this a heavy, preachy, lecturing novel to make someone feel bad. But you can bet this novel will be rich in theme. I personally feel humor is one of the most powerful ways to strike home with heavy messages. My favorite novels are the ones that make me cry while I'm laughing.

I hate to use the word *messages* because it implies a heavy agenda for writing a book. Some people do have heavy agendas, though, and some of those novels are fantastic. A novel like *The Help* has some very intense themes, and, I would say, a heavy message about racism. So does *To Kill a Mockingbird*. Heavy themes, heavy messages, aren't essentially bad. But if you examine closely the great novels that have thematic messages, they are done beautifully through the thoughts, actions, and speech of their characters. You won't find pages of pontificating on the evils of racism in those novels.

Pitfalls of Working Themes into Your Story

So watch out for pitfalls when trying to develop themes in a story. Writers sometimes try to cram theme in their stories by preaching, lecturing, and long explanations—either via the characters or as author intrusion. You'll notice in the best movies and novels that have strong themes that those discussions centering directly on theme will feel organic to what is happening in the plot and to the characters. Theme should manifest as a result of the events unfolding in your story that force characters to stand up, oppose, complain, dare, risk, turn away,

87

stop, prevent, speak out, shut up—you get the point. Readers get the theme by watching you *show* (not tell) the story.

Although it's possible that theme may naturally or accidentally come through as a writer creates scenes and plays out her story, writing a novel with the intention of establishing, developing, and capitalizing on theme will make for a much better, more focused novel.

I hope this has given you some inspiring ways to approach your novel's themes. Think of themes as topics, issues, concerns. Find the heart of your story's ethics and morals. Brainstorm by asking questions of your characters and their passions.

As you read the novels you love, jot down the themes you see presented. Then pay attention to how the writer brings them out. Use a yellow highlighter, and mark up every line that speaks to theme (on a used paperback and not that special first-edition hardcover version!). You'll be glad you did.

Moving On . . .

We've now completed our look at the first four of twelve pillars—the four crucial corner pillars of novel construction. I've spent more than a third of this book on just these, but for good reason. I hope you see how, by constructing your story via focusing on these first four pillars, your novel will hold up to scrutiny and will be well supported by those sturdy corner pillars.

I've added the fourth inspection checklist. Photocopy the checklist or type this link into your Internet browser: http://bit.ly/1A0ZQsu. May these checklists help you construct a solid novel.

Inspection Checklist #4
Theme with a Heart

Question #1:

Ask yourself, "What is my novel about?" Now really ask, "What is my novel really about?" Answer it here, centering on the theme, not the plot.

Question #2:

List (or create) 10 places your theme is explored in your novel—by whom, how, and in what situation. Can you bring the theme out stronger?

Question #3:

What iconic scene in your novel showcases (or will showcase) the heart of your theme? Blow it up as big as you can so it's the key scene.

Question #4:

What are your protagonist's passionate views on this theme, and how do they tie in with her core need and goal for the story?

Question #5:

Who challenges the views, actions, and beliefs of your protagonist in a way that involves your thematic elements? Make their opinions even stronger with higher stakes and greater conflict.

Question #6:

How is your theme showcased in the climactic scenes of your book? Can you make the stakes higher and the choices harder for your protagonist?

Question #7:

If you can't identify any themes, can you come up with three thematic topics to tie in with key decisions your protagonist makes? Make the issues more important and work that into the scenes.

Question #8:

What wounds/past hurts have formed your characters? Can you find ways to tweak them to link thematically together?

Question #9:

Is your theme strongly emphasized in your final chapter? Yes? Bring it out even more. No? Find a way to home in on it so it brings depth to your novel.

Question #10:

Find (or think of) 5 key scenes that showcase your theme. Print them out or compile in a new document. Can you blow the theme up bigger in each one? Give it a try!

Question #11:

Go back to your opening scene and ask: Does this scene introduce the key themes of my story? Is it really the best scene to open with that will do so?

Question #12:

Can you come up with a line your protagonist can repeat at least three times in the novel (best if that includes the first and last scenes) that will voice his feelings about the theme?

Chapter 12: Revisiting the Four Corner Pillars of Novel Construction

Before I plow ahead to pillar #5, I want to step back a moment and take another holistic look at these four corner pillars. I mentioned that you need to work on all four at once. You don't have to start with any particular one or go in any order. Think more of blending all four together, adding bits to each one as you brainstorm these components.

Mind mapping these four pillars together will help you strengthen them all until you have a truly strong and lasting support. Then you can move on to the other eight support pillars.

Let's Review Those Four Pillars

We first looked at Concept with a Kicker. You can't just run with an idea or a basic premise. You need to create the kind of story concept that will make people excited to learn more about your novel just by hearing the one-line story summation you've come up with. Your story concept, all by its lonesome, should get people saying "wow." So what is a one-line story concept all about?

Michael Hauge, screenwriting consultant and best-selling author of *Writing Screenplays That Sell*, encourages writers to come up with one sentence that tells the concept—and that sentence is all about the next pillar we looked at—the Protagonist with a Goal. When you can write that one sentence to describe your story by expressing the protagonist's goal with the emphasis on the kicker—or what makes your story so unique—you will be on track.

Remember, your premise should ask an intriguing "what if?" question, and although your concept may be one that's been used many times by many writers, *yours* takes a unique approach, or is framed in unusual or intriguing circumstances (setting/locale or world/local events), or features characters whose careers or passions frame the concept in a fresh, compelling way.

And along with noting the protagonist and his goal in that one-sentence story concept, you need to identify the third pillar: the central Conflict with High Stakes.

Note how these one-sentence story concepts from recent movie releases include those elements (taken from Netflix.com):

- *Maleficent*: "Turning the classic fairy tale 'Sleeping Beauty' on its head, this fantasy drama retells the story from the point of view of evil godmother Maleficent. While defending her homeland from invaders, the young Maleficent is dealt a cruel blow by fate." The kicker is having the evil antagonist be the protagonist of the story.

- *The Giver*: "In a future society called The Community, pain, war, and disease have been eradicated, as have individuality and free will. When a teenager named Jonas learns the truth about the real world, he must decide whether to reveal all or remain quiet." Note the high stakes, the protagonist's goal. The "what if?" is tied in with what Jonas will do with the secrets he uncovers. Also clear are potential themes. The unusual setting "frames" the well-used basic plot in a new setting.

- *Non-Stop*: "On a commercial flight at 40,000 feet, federal air marshal Bill Marks starts receiving text messages from a threatening blackmailer who claims he's on the airplane too. Can Marks identify his camouflaged adversary before he [assuming this means the blackmailer and not Marks] begins killing passengers?" No need to comment on the unique setting for this cop-chasing-crook story, or the kind of high stakes involved.

- *The Fault in our Stars*: "Teenager Hazel, who has pushed people away since her cancer diagnosis, reluctantly joins a support group, where she bonds with a boy named Gus. Together, they face the challenge of building a relationship under the shadow of terminal illness." Here's a great scenario for a typical love story—a Concept with a Kicker that has potential for a lot of emotional high stakes and themes. Falling in love knowing you could lose the one you love—or you could die and cause your loved one pain? That's huge.

- *Snowpiercer.* "The Earth's remaining inhabitants are confined to a single train circling the globe as revolution brews among the class-divided cars." Again, a unique setting/situation to give a twist to the commonplace plot of man against man and exploring themes about class.

I hope you are starting to see how you need to be able to nail your Concept with a Kicker, Protagonist with a Goal, and Conflict with High Stakes in just one sentence. If you can't, that may mean you haven't built a strong pillar (or two or three) and you need to get to work before you go any further.

Theme is not often mentioned in a one-sentence concept, but it isn't hard to come up with lots of thematic ideas for any of the above stories. Theme is up to the writer, and just about any story can showcase a variety of themes. As we explored, theme is what is at the heart of your story. And that is always tied in with what goal the protagonist is after. So when you summarize your story concept, think what themes make your story unique, and what gives your story heart.

Remember: A Concept Is Not Just a Cool Idea

There is a huge difference between this: "A teenage girl in a dystopian future society has to struggle to survive and keep her family alive" and this: "A teenage girl conscripted to participate in deadly games foments rebellion that eventually destroys the oppressive government in order to provide hope and a future for those she loves." *The Hunger Games* series is about Katniss, the heroine. It's her story.

I agree with Michael Hauge when he says every great story is about *someone*, not something. Every great story has one main character the reader roots for and cares about—a character with a visible goal she strives to reach. It may sound simple—yes, it is! But you would be surprised how few novels by aspiring authors have this element in it at all.

The fourth pillar—Theme with a Heart—is the glue that holds the whole story together. *The Hunger Games* is really about a whole lot more than a girl trying to survive. It delves into issues of loyalty, self-sacrifice, human rights and inequity, how people should govern other people, and ultimately forgiveness. A lot of themes on many levels throughout the three-book series.

You Gotta Have Conflict and High Stakes

I recently saw the movie *Divergent* and read the first book (which is similar enough to the movie). If you said that *Divergent* was about a dystopian society in which everyone gets put into one of five different groups and has to conform to the rules of that group, you wouldn't even be close to the concept and kicker.

The book (and film) is about Beatrice (Tris). The central conflict is centered on one faction led by one woman, who is intent on using another of the factions to commit genocide (essentially). Tris, the protagonist, has a goal that emerges as she trains to become an accepted member of Dauntless. She learns of this plot to kill all the members of her former faction (Abnegation) and hence must strive toward that goal—to stop this massacre and, while doing so, save her family. We see fairly late in the movie and book this goal emerge (not at the traditional 25% mark), but the conflicts and tension she faces in her training—building allies and making enemies—play an important part. The themes, here too, grow organically from what the protagonist's goal is.

Don't forget: great novels have high stakes. And what are the stakes? What your protagonist must be willing to risk, what danger he will be willing to face, in order to reach his goal. When what *he's* passionate about is threatened, those are high stakes.

And Finally Theme . . .

Remember, theme is the protagonist's goal made universal. The things your character cares most about, which is why he is going after that goal, are things lots of people care about. So if your protagonist is not really concerned about anything that concerns most people in the world, you might need to spend some time working on that pillar to give him a passion and concern for something that will resonate with other humans on the planet.

I'm not talking specifics here. We looked at Amy in *Fly Away Home* and how she cared about a flock of geese—which isn't something a lot of people stay up nights worrying about. What she cared about was compassion and survival. Her goal is made universal, for it resonates with us all on those bigger issues—the themes. She could have been saving dogs, unwanted children, or rainforests. It's a variation of the age-old standard plot: man against society.

We resonate with characters who are going through tough situations and have to draw strength and courage to face obstacles. We respect characters who are assertive, humorous, humble, innovative, smart, clever, and who refuse to give up. We care about characters who care about more than just themselves. It may sound silly, but I think we read *to care*.

So as you write or rewrite your novel, spend a serious amount of time working on these four corner pillars. Go through all the questions on the inspection checklists, and see where your structure is weak.

Get Help if You Are Stuck

If you are stuck and can't quite get one of the pillars strong enough, enlist the help of other authors or a writing coach to help you work out the kinks and maybe help you find some better building materials. Don't settle for so-so or trust that the ideas will come later on as you write the book. Build a framework, then work within it. Think of your novel as a house, and don't keep nailing siding onto a weak, flimsy structure.

I speak truth when I say such a weak structure will not hold up. It won't. You will have to tear all that siding off and then rebuild the framework. Maybe that's okay with you and part of your style, your creative process. But why waste weeks, months, or years of your life tearing your hair out trying to rework a novel that isn't structurally sound (and that may need to be demolished)? Why not be smart and start with the right building materials and a proven-sturdy structure?

Don't answer that. Just think about it. And about what you could do with all that time you could save . . .

Part 2: The Eight Secondary Pillars of Novel Support

Pillar #5: Plot and Subplots in a String of Scenes

Chapter 13: Plots and Subplots That Serve as Vehicles for Your Story

Ah, now we're getting somewhere, some of you may be thinking. We're finally going to look deeply at plot. And rightly so. A great, strong plot is essential for building a terrific novel. There is no excuse for a writer of any novel to sacrifice good plot for the sake of anything—art, character study, or an important message. Without plot, you have no story. Period. So don't misunderstand me if I *appear* to underemphasize plot at times.

Yes, I'm a "character-driven" novelist. My novels are centered on my characters—what they need, want, fear, and strive for. I feel every well-constructed novel must be character-driven in that way. But not at the expense of good plot. Every little bit of every scene has to serve the needs of the plot.

So, What Is Plot?

But what is plot? I said this in an earlier chapter: plot *isn't* one of the four essential corner pillars of novel construction. Why? Because plot is the *vehicle* for the other pillars. Plot is what happens in a string of scenes, one scene after the other. Plot itself isn't a pillar of novel construction, but the way scenes are constructed to unfold the plot is.

To veer away from my construction theme, think about plot as a train trip. Scene 1 is the departure station. Your story begins on page 1 with an opening scene. Your novel ends at "The End"—the final scene, the destination point. Each scene might be likened to a stop along the way, one stop after another, that keeps you moving to the destination. The plot is the train ride from start to finish. It is not the story; it's what gets you from point A to point Z.

A Direct Route

If you got on a train in Los Angeles and planned to go to Denver, Colorado, in a timely fashion, would it make sense for you to mosey over to Seattle, then pop up into Canada, head to New York, maybe backtrack to Los Angeles, then journey through Texas, and maybe (finally) end up in Colorado (if you are lucky and remembered that was where you wanted to go all along)? I think not.

Yet, believe it or not, that is what a lot of novels are like (and often with a lot of backtracking to earlier stops, by way of backstory, that confuses the story flow). A trip like the one I mentioned might be a whole lot of fun if you had no real destination in mind. If you didn't care at all where you went, how quickly, how much time and money you spent, or where you ended up. Some novels give that same impression to me—the writer really didn't have any idea where he meant to go or end up.

But let's pretend that you, the novelist, have a clear journey in mind. You want your protagonist to start at point A and end up at point Z at the end of the book without making crazy, irrational, boring, meaningless, or confusing stops along the way. Readers want a clear ride from beginning to end. I don't mean smooth, without bumps. Conflict promises a bumpy ride. The wilder the ride, the better (no shock absorbers on your train!).

Don't Confuse Your Reader

But the last thing a novelist wants is for a reader to be scratching her head wondering what the heck the book is about, what the protagonist wants, or where the story is going. If you give someone a train ticket and tell them they are going to New York, they expect to end up in New York.

What am I saying here? That the author makes a promise to the reader by way of genre, book description, and back-cover copy. That promise is also then set up clearly for the reader in the opening scenes.

99

That is the "ticket" you give to your readers telling them what type of "trip" they expect when they start reading page 1 to the end.

What Does All This Have to Do with Plot?

Everything. What's important is *how* the plot is constructed, not what the plot *is*.

By now you should understand that plot is not an idea, concept, or premise. If you've developed your Concept with a Kicker, and have figured out clearly what your Conflict with High Stakes is, as well as your themes embodied in the protagonist being passionate about some outer goal pressed by inner motivation, you have the necessary framework to write a great novel. The plot, then, will be the *execution* of all this.

And how is that done? How do you take all those great elements you now have in place and somehow turn it into a killer novel?

By constructing scenes.

Move Forward, One Stop at a Time

Each stop along that train ride is a scene. Each scene follows the one prior. All scenes string together over a set period of time (the capsule of time your entire novel covers, which usually will be a matter of weeks or months at most, unless you are writing some epic saga). For the most part, for most novels, that means moving forward, step by step, in time. Moving forward naturally in time is the easiest and smoothest way to tell a story.

I'm not saying novels should never have any flashbacks or backstory, because that would not be true. Many novels benefit greatly from scenes that jump back in time at key moments for a specific effect and purpose. Other novels feature multiple timelines—showing, in a sense, two or more train rides, each train reaching different destinations but for the same purpose. What purpose? To show how the protagonist goes after his goal, and maybe what the consequences of his choices are.

But for now, let's just focus on the basic structure for a novel, and that's moving forward, one increment at a time, scene by scene. I would encourage beginning novelists to try to master scene construction and stringing scenes together in proper time order *first*, before attempting a novel that requires skipping around in time.

Constructing a solid novel that moves back and forth from the present to the past, or maybe into the future, is not easy. I'm not saying it shouldn't be done. I love novels that have multiple timelines, and I've written quite a few myself. But I made the mistake in my first novel of having a lot of full flashback scenes to fill in backstory, and that novel will never be published.

I have yet to see more than a handful of novels by beginning writers (out of hundreds of manuscripts) that feature a nonlinear timeline that are truly well structured. So my advice? Master scene structure and laying out plot in a string of scenes before attempting something complicated.

Start Thinking about Plot Differently

If you can tweak your definition about plot from here on out, you will start seeing plot in a very different light. You will stop thinking, "What's my plot about?" and start thinking, "How am I structuring my plot?"

Stop confusing plot with concept. Once you have your concept solid, your job is to come up with a string of scenes that will link smoothly together, from point A to point Z, to tell the story you mean to tell—in the most succinct, concise, and compelling way possible.

And I will tell you right now: what I see is *the* biggest problem in novels is failure to know how to construct a scene. Scenes convey the plot (story line). If they are not built right, and do not achieve what's needed—each and every scene—your story will collapse.

So we're going to look at scene structure a bit, and then we'll examine subplots and how they fit into novel structure. Regardless of how many plot layers you have in a novel, every scene has to "serve the needs" of the primary plot. And the primary plot centers on the protagonist's pursuit of his outer motivation (visible goal). And how do you write a plot? One scene at a time.

I know this way of looking at plot is different from what most writing instructors teach, but I've found that it has helped hundreds of my editing clients. Too many writers have great plot ideas and elements, but few have a clue how to take all those great bits and turn them into a great novel. They often succumb to the false belief that their cool concept will somehow convert into a masterpiece.

The Daunting Chasm

There seems to be a huge chasm looming in front of many writers—with no bridge across. On one side stands the writer with all these terrific ideas, characters, themes, and conflict. On the other side is this nebulous thing called a coherent finished novel ready to jump to the top of the best-seller lists. This seems to be the drop-off point for most novelists—ending in a long, painful fall to the bottom of the chasm.

Writers, when facing this chasm, often just take a running leap with eyes closed and hope they make it to the other side. Really, this is just what their manuscript seems like. Scenes thrown together on a whim, which the author hopes will somehow fashion into a sturdy bridge that will span the chasm and, phew, get her (and readers) to the other side.

And sometimes it kind of works. She might end up with a partially functioning bridge that someone, if traversing carefully around the missing boards and weak materials, might be able to cross—once or twice—before total collapse.

You Need a Well-Constructed Bridge

What's the point of this allegory? Swinging back to our motif—construction—we have to consider structure. Building materials. Methods of construction. You don't hammer nails into siding using a paintbrush. You don't weld copper piping for hot-water lines with Silly Putty. You don't use paper towels for roof underlayment.

So how does this apply to unfolding a plot? I mentioned that scenes must be strung together, one at a time, moving forward in time to tell a story. Plot is the vehicle for your story, and scenes are the vehicle for the plot. But, like everything else in novel construction, scenes need to be structured in a way that ensures solid framework for your plot.

What's the Problem Here?

I think the biggest problem regarding scene structure in most manuscripts is writers feel they 1) know instinctively what a scene is and how to construct one or 2) don't know how to structure scenes but don't think there is any specific "rule" to constructing them or 3) don't really care to learn how to structure scenes.

I would like to think #3 doesn't ever apply, but a lot of manuscripts seem to have scenes thoughtlessly plopped in here and there (or everywhere) without much forethought or purpose. However, I feel most writers who are actually plotting their novels carefully ahead of time and have scenes that don't evidence much forethought or purpose fall victim to issue #2.

If only someone had sat down with them before they spent years writing their epic novel and shown them scene structure. I can't tell you how many clients I've had tell me they wish they'd understood this basic structure *before* they started writing. I can't tell you how many because I long ago lost count.

No, There Isn't Just One Way

This may lead you to believe there is just one way to construct a scene. Of course there isn't. Just as there isn't one set way to write a novel. The fun part about being a novelist is you get to be creative and original and express yourself any which way you want. The difficult part about being a novelist is if you veer too far from time-tested, traditionally accepted novel structure, you take the chance of novel failure.

The same is true regarding scene construction. I'm going to give you some very basic "rules" about scene structure that serve many successful writers well. That most great writing instructors agree on. That most commercially successful authors swear by. Now, once you learn all this, if you want to veer, go ahead—veer to your heart's content.

Here's the Secret

Just know this: if you can really get the hang of scene structure, you'll be well on your way to solid novel construction. It's one of the most important tools in your writer's toolbox. Without it, you may as well piece your plot together with duct tape. Yes, I know you can use duct tape for pretty much anything, but trust me—it will not hold your plot together. This just may be the only thing duct tape *isn't* good for!

Chapter 14: Breaking Down Scene Structure into Bite-Sized Bits

I mentioned that the greatest issue I come across while critiquing and editing more than two hundred partial and complete manuscripts a year is this: poor understanding and execution of scene structure. So let's look at the key components to scene structure to understand just what goes into this essential pillar of novel construction.

Scenes Must Move the Story Along

There are lots of ways to construct a scene, but most people will agree there is one main objective for a scene and that's to "move the story along." I put that in quotes because it's vague. Yes, we want to move the story along, bit by bit, one scene at a time. But that should raise some questions. How many "bits" should you reveal in each scene? How long should a scene be? Where should you start a scene, and when should you end it?

There are many excellent books that detail traditional plot structure, but we're not going to turn off onto that track, as it would take way too many pages to cover and doesn't really fall under the scope of pillar construction. But it's good to be aware of the generally accepted plot development most novels follow. There is much more to this, with specific turning points at defined places in a story, but to keep it simple, this is how your plot timeline might look if laid out like a train trip such as the one I described earlier:

- The starting point of your timeline features your opening scenes that set up the premise and the world of your story, and showcase your protagonist and his life, needs, dreams, and ordinary world he lives in.

- Note at around the 10% mark there will be an important event or disturbance that will start your protagonist in a direction that kicks off the story and supports your premise.

- At around the 25% mark, some key development occurs in your story that cements the goal for your character.

- The midpoint at 50% to the 75% section is where your protagonist makes progress toward his goal and faces more and more obstacles along his way. The train ride gets bumpier and steeper.

- Somewhere between the 75% and 90% mark of your novel, your protagonist is going to either reach his goal or fail. This is the climax of your novel.

- The last 5-10% of your novel is the quick wrap-up of the story and loose ends.

Your novel may not follow this convention exactly, but if your structure doesn't look anything like this, you may want to take some time to study books on plot structure to help you lay out those many scenes you hope will unfold your story in a clear and meaningful way.

So the way you "move the story along" is to create scenes that string together, each scene helping to reveal plot and character but for a specific purpose. However, if your scenes aren't built well, the "train ride" is going to drag, maybe even stall. Readers may end up frustrated and decide to jump off and hoof it back home, abandon the journey.

The Essential Characteristics of a Scene

In order to build strong scenes, writers need to understand the key ingredients. Just what goes into that cement mixer to create sturdy scene pillars?

Let me give you this definition of a scene by Jordan Rosenfeld in her book *Make a Scene*. It's the best definition I've found and the one we're going to break down and carefully look at. Rosenfeld says: "Scenes are capsules in which compelling characters undertake significant actions in a vivid and memorable way that allows the events to feel as though they are happening in real time."

So let's break her definition down:

- *Capsule*: The word *capsule* implies a limited, compressed period of time. Scenes start in one moment, in present action, and move forward in real time, then end—without breaking up the scene into other times, places, or POVs.

- *Compelling characters undertaking significant actions*: Scenes need to feature compelling characters, all of whom must have significant impact on the protagonist, acting as either an ally (reflection character), a romance interest, or an antagonist. All should have core needs and goals that either help or hinder the protagonist from reaching her goal. And the protagonist's actions in a scene must also be important in relation to her goal.

- *Vivid and memorable*: Use as much sensory detail in a scene to bring it to life without bogging down with too much unnecessary description. And what makes a scene memorable is giving it a high moment—which reveals something essential about the characters and/or plot.

- *Happening in real time*: Backstory, long flashbacks, and excessive narration stop the present action and interrupt the pacing and flow of the scene. Author intrusion is jarring and unwelcome. Just show, don't tell, events as they happen. Briefly summarize what isn't important enough to show but needs to be conveyed.

If you've been reading my blog or other writing craft books these last few years or have attended any workshops I've taught, you'll be very familiar with my emphasis on the "high moment" in a scene. Great stories have great moments, and adept writers will ensure that every single scene in their novel has a high moment or some important plot point or character insight revealed at the "climax" of that scene. Usually that means starting a scene just a little bit before that high moment and building to it.

If you learn nothing else from me, learn this: your scene must have a point to it or it shouldn't be in your novel.

Learn Scene Structure by Asking Questions

My advice for all writers is this: take the time to really learn scene structure. Study the novels of great writers who know how to do this well. Observe at what point in time they begin a scene. See how they build to a high moment then end the scene. Figure out how much time passes during that scene. Notice how the scene is shown through the POV character—which means that the scene is restricted by what this character sees, thinks, knows, and experiences as the scene plays out—and how the action is moving in real time, in the present, leaving out unessential or boring information that does not help to reveal character or plot.

Take a look at your scenes. There are a number of key questions you can ask about your scenes to determine if they're structured soundly, and I've put these questions together in a bonus checklist so that you can analyze scenes in your novel and see if they "hold up."

Writers don't need to wing it, or guess or hope their scenes are structured correctly. Just as in novel construction, there are time-tested rules to ensure a powerful scene. If you construct your scenes with strong "materials" and string them together in a smooth time flow, you will provide the proper framework for your plot and subplots.

Here's your bonus scene structure checklist! To download and print out copies, click on the link or type this into a web browser: http://bit.ly/1yQEu43.

Scene Structure Checklist

Examine each of your scenes. The more you can check off the list per scene, the better!

_____ My scene has a strong opening line (hook) that grabs the reader.

_____ My scene has a beginning, middle, high point, and end (hanging or resolved).

_____ My scene is important to the plot (and I can explain exactly why and how that is).

_____ My scene helps reveal something new about the characters or plot.

_____ My scene starts in the middle of action in present time and moves forward.

_____ My scene gives a brief nod to setting through the character's POV.

_____ My scene stays in one POV the whole time and makes clear who the POV character is right away (preferably in the first two lines).

_____ My scene has dialog that has been compressed and distilled, which provides bits of important info or backstory as well as reveals character.

_____ My scene has brief bits of narrative, but not more than a few lines in one place before it switches to either internal thinking or dialog.

_____ My scene is full of sensory detail: smells, sound, textures, weather, etc.

_____ My scene clearly indicates how much time has passed since the last scene with these characters as well as the previous scene in my novel (if different).

_____ My scene evokes a rich setting to which my POV character reacts and responds.

_____ My scene's high moment advances the plot in an important way.

_____ My scene begins in a different kind of way than the scene before (usually).

_____ My scene has some element of surprise, twist, or interesting motif that makes it meaningful and helps bring across the themes of the novel.

_____ My scene is full of inner and/or outer conflict to some degree that complicates the plot and either aids or hinders my main character's attempt to reach her goal (outer motivation in the story).

_____ My scene has no dull parts; I've taken them all out! I've resisted the urge to explain!

_____ My scene has no extra words or clunky writing; I've gone through and cut as much as I could so that less is more and every word is just right and needed.

Chapter 15: Mastering the Passing of Time in Novel Scenes

Scene structure is an essential concept writers must grasp in order to construct solid, fluid novels. I chose that word *fluid* because I feel readers want something akin to a smooth read. I don't mean specifically a linear story in which every moment passes in time the same way. I mean the story being told is easy to follow because the scenes string together in a clear flow of time, each giving the sense of real time passing, right here, right now.

This may be a tricky concept for some to grasp, so bear with me a bit. In a film, there are lots of techniques available to the filmmaker to make time appear to slow down or speed up. Novelists have to use creative ways of wording to show these same effects. But scenes, essentially, are all about showing significant action happening in real time—the way time passes for us as we go through our lives. The variable, however, is linked to the POV character, who is experiencing and showing the action through her eyes.

What do I mean? Well, time is *perceived* by each of us individually and differently. Sometimes time seems to drag. Other times it goes so fast that we can't keep up with what is happening around us. Perception is the key.

Now, let's take this whole concept and think about scene construction.

Great Scenes Are Capsules

In each scene in your novel, you cover a specific period of time. There is a starting point in time and a point when the scene ends. That scene might cover a period of one minute or one hour. Why might it

110

vary so much? Because whatever needs to take place in that scene does so via the perception of the POV character.

Let's say you have a scene in which your hero is dangling by a rope over a cliff. The bad guys have shot him, and he's bleeding profusely. The whole scene is his struggle to pull himself up onto the ledge and to safety. You may feel as if that isn't a whole scene. It certainly can be, if it has a beginning, middle, and end (which can, literally, be a cliffhanger).

So, you could have a rich, compelling scene that might even take ten long pages to show your hero pulling himself up onto a ledge covering maybe three minutes of real time. In another scene, three minutes may pass in the blink of an eye. It's all about the character's perception and what's happening to him.

However, it's very hard to create an efficient, effective scene if too much time passes and too many things happen that are not clearly built as an individual high moment. Scenes like that will feel pointless and will usually drag. Readers are looking for that point of your scene, often subconsciously. If they get to the end of it and you haven't made a point, they will feel gyped, even if they don't realize it.

Adjust the Pacing of Your Novel So It Reflects Real Life

When we're in danger, or anxiously waiting for something, or in great pain, time seems to drag. When we're in the midst of an exciting competition or other fast action, time sometimes seems to race along at the speed of light. The challenge for the novelist, then, is to keep time moving forward by showing significant action in real time but tweaked appropriately for the POV character's perception.

This will greatly affect the pacing of your novel, which should vary just as time in real life varies. You should have scenes that feel as if they are moving fast and others in which it seems time is dragging, even painfully slowly.

Genre plays a part, as does the position of a scene in the novel. Fast-action suspense scenes speed up the closer they get to the climax. But you could have a suspenseful survival story, perhaps about someone cresting Mt. Everest, that slows down to a grueling crawl in the scenes leading to the climax.

Just because *time* is moving slowly, that doesn't mean the pacing or novel itself is dragging. Don't get confused about that. Suspense and pacing are all tied up with the reader caring—worrying—about what will happen to their beloved protagonist next. That is what creates suspense, for the most part.

String Those Capsules Together

Playing with the sense of time passing is one of my favorite things to do in a novel. I love the way time flows and ebbs and stalls and rushes in my life. Time takes us on a wild ride, an erratic adventure through the ups and downs of existence. Time should be that way for your characters—and readers—as well. But with that said, scenes need to be strung together as capsules of time, like a string of pearls, each unfolding the story and providing meaningful, *important* information to help push the plot and characters forward in a compelling way.

It's all about showing a scene playing out in real time. Readers do not want to be told what happens to the characters or how they feel. They don't want story summaries in the guise of scenes. They want to watch, in real time, what is happening to the character—but through the POV character's eyes and perception. Once you really get that, you will discover how fun it is to manipulate time as you play out your plot.

Chapter 16: How to Add Meaningful Subplots to Your Novel

When I first started considering writing novels, I found the idea of subplots daunting. I knew I needed to put them in, but I really had no idea how, why, or in what manner subplots played a role in novel structure.

Subplots are everywhere. We see them in the movies we watch, and they are usually in every novel we read. We may instinctively know how they work in story structure. I always thought they were inserted to give some depth to the overall story, whether movie or novel. And that is one purpose for a subplot. But writers need to be careful not to throw any old subplot into a story in the hope that it will just add some interest. If you keep in mind that everything that goes into your novel must serve the advancement and complication of the main plot, you will fare well.

Subplots Serve a Purpose

What do I mean by "serve the advancement" of the main plot? This brings us back to our four support corner pillars. The main plot is all about a protagonist going after a goal in the midst of conflict and high stakes. That's the essence of the main plot's purpose—to be a vehicle for this character and her objective in the story.

So, if you keep in mind that any subplots (additional plotlines) you create should *add to the main plot in a meaningful way*, that can help you come up with some interesting and helpful subplots.

Subplots can involve your protagonist and/or your secondary characters. Regardless, whatever side stories you weave into your novel, they need to impact your protagonist.

I have read numerous novels, some by best-selling authors, who have subplots thrown into their stories that don't fit at all. These subplots feel dropped in as noise and distraction, and I've sometimes found myself skimming pages to get past them in order to get back to the gripping main plot. That's a bad thing.

In addition to being irrelevant to the novel's purpose and premise, they are often boring, featuring mundane concerns and activities that don't add anything of interest. And that makes for a dissatisfied reader.

Plot Layers That Mimic Real Life

I came up with a concept of plot layers, and I've written some detailed posts on this that can help writers get how to layer plots (which you can search for on my blog Live Write Thrive), but I'll briefly summarize the idea.

We want our characters to have lives that feel real and similar to our own. Novels should be portraying a slice of real life (but just more interesting, we hope). Our lives are multilayered with different objectives or goals, and if you look at your life in these terms, you can identify numerous goals you are pursuing each day, year in and year out.

Some of these goals are big and cover years of your life. The "big" goal in your life may be to find a person to marry, raise a family, get a college degree or a great job, or travel the world. Much of your time, effort, and thinking may wrap around a big goal such as one of these.

However, life is not one main plot. Life is full of short-term and long-term goals. You may have some more immediate goals of trying to write a paper for a class or put a presentation together for your job. You may have the goal of losing ten pounds over the next few months (or years). These are also goals that you could think of as "subplots" in your life.

And then you have small daily goals, such as getting the grocery shopping done or finding a company to shampoo your carpets. Life is made up of layers of goals. Layers of plot in the story of your life. Some goals may be boring; others may be exciting. But it's all part of life.

How to Show Ordinary Life in a Meaningful Way

Now, since you don't want your novel or characters to be boring or involved in boring activities, this begs the question: How do you make your characters' lives real and mirroring real life if you don't have similar kinds of plot layers, including some of the daily mundane, boring ones?

Glad you asked. And this, to me, is the secret to writing great plots and subplots in a novel. Make this the word you associate with subplots: *complicate*. If you make it your objective to use your subplots to complicate your story, that is a first strong construction step. But that doesn't mean you want to throw in side stories that are only messy situations.

The best purpose for subplots is to enrich, deepen, and help advance the main plot and reveal character motivation. So with every subplot you add in (and often, the more the better), utilizing any number of secondary characters, find a way for each additional story line to be a complication. For whom? Ultimately, for your protagonist. For, even if the subplot is about another character, the impact of what that character is going through *has to affect your protagonist*. (We'll examine secondary characters next when we go over that pillar of novel construction, so I'll hold back on delving too deeply into this now.)

By making sure all the secondary plots tie in, enhance, and, most importantly, *complicate* the main plot concerning the protagonist going after his visible goal, you will be working with strong construction materials.

Don't throw random subplots into your novel just for filler or because you think they are neat ideas. They really must serve a purpose in your story. Sure, make some of them entertaining, even providing comic relief. Subplots really help to bring out your characters and all their issues, and they help make your characters clash, which, to me, is the best reason for layering plots.

Showcase Your Themes with Subplots

The key to coming up with great subplots is to keep in mind your themes for your novel. Subplots are great devices for showcasing theme, with your secondary characters embodying an opposing view from that of your protagonist.

Take some time to brainstorm lots of ideas for your subplots. Think about the allies and antagonists in your novel, who are there to help or hinder your main character in reaching her objective for the book. Give them plot layers that will help bring out your themes, challenge your protagonist, and, of course, *complicate* your story.

Subplots Require Thought and Intention

To summarize: If you make it your aim to make it as hard as possible for your hero to reach his goal, subplots can be very useful in this way. Don't settle for a boring, wimpy subplot as filler. A great subplot can turn a good novel into a great one. This one pillar of novel construction—Plot and Subplots in a String of Scenes—requires careful attention and deliberation.

Structure your scenes correctly, creating capsules of time in which significant action takes place. Those scenes will be the vehicle for your plot and subplots, to take your reader from the beginning to the end of your story in a riveting, cohesive manner.

You many feel I brushed past the huge topic of plot because I didn't go in depth on all the specifics of constructing your plot. Although it's crucial that construction be done carefully, it would take an entire book to explore sufficiently. For our immediate purposes, though, the key pillar that must be built well relies on efficient, tight scene construction as a framework to support your plot, so that's what we've been focusing on.

I hope this look at scene structure and subplots has helped you construct a strong pillar for your novel.

Ready for your next checklist? Photocopy the checklist or type this link into your Internet browser: http://bit.ly/1qOa5kf.

Next, we move into exploring pillar #6: Secondary Characters with Their Own Needs. This will segue nicely with what we've just gone over about subplots.

Inspection Checklist #5
Plot and Subplot in a String of Scenes

Question #1:

Take the time to look at each of your scenes. Does each scene have a beginning, middle, high point, and end? If not, rewrite so they do or consider deleting.

Question #2:

Does every scene advance your main plot by revealing new, important info about character or the plot or by adding complications or obstacles for your protagonist in reaching her goal?

Question #3:

Does every scene have an opening hook that grabs the reader? A great last line that leaves the scene hanging or wraps it up just right?

Question #4:

Does every scene clearly set up where, when, and who is the focus of the scene right away? Show how much time has passed since the last scene? Establish and stay with the POV character?

Question #5:

Does every scene start in the middle of something happening? Have you deleted all the boring, nonessential action and words that make your scene drag?

Question #6:

Sum up your main plot in one sentence. Does it clearly show your protagonist's visible goal for the novel as well as the central conflict? Rework it until your plot objective is clear.

Question #7:

What are the two main subplots for your protagonist (Plots B and C)? In what ways do they complicate the main plot? Enrich your themes?

Question #8:

What are the subplots you've created for two of your secondary characters? In what ways do they complicate the main plot and showcase your theme? Help or hinder your protagonist?

Question #9:

List three ways your subplots bring out your themes. Can you find a way in five scenes to bring out the theme even more?

Question #10:

Do you have a subplot that involves a secondary character that clashes with your protagonist's goal? Can you make it bigger, worse?

Question #11:

What minor subplot do you have for your protagonist? Can you find ways in those scenes to aggravate the situation so that it pushes your protagonist over the edge?

Question #12:

`Find your three weakest scenes in which not much is happening. Can you salvage these by infusing a twist, an important high moment, a revelation or insight for your character?

Pillar #6: Secondary Characters with Their Own Needs

Chapter 17: Secondary Characters Have a Life of Their Own

We're now getting into another one of my favorite topics: secondary characters. This pillar in your novel is so important, it could almost be a corner support pillar. In this course exploring the twelve key pillars of novel construction, we've spent a lot of time looking at your main character—your protagonist—and we've dabbled a little into the role secondary characters play in your story. But there is so much more to this important pillar.

The importance of secondary characters in your novel cannot be overemphasized. They are crucial to your story—unless you are writing about a protagonist in isolation, which, as I mentioned earlier, is a unique kind of story. And novels about one person off alone are challenging to write because of the dearth of a "supporting cast."

The Need for a Supporting Cast

Having other characters in your novel makes it much easier to construct a strong story. Why? Because these characters provide support and opposition to your protagonist as he goes after his goal for the book. By now you've had it drilled into you that your novel should be about one main character who is after something. We looked at the five main types of goals "heroes" pursue in a story, and many of the sections you've read in this book emphasize the fact that everything in a novel centers on the protagonist's goal.

If you keep this in mind, you will create additional characters that will either help or hinder your protagonist. We took a look at how subplots are worked into stories with this same objective. The subplots of both the main and secondary characters should be all about advancing the main plot. How do you "advance" a plot? By helping or hindering the protagonist as he goes after his goal.

Yes, I am being repetitive for a reason. Too many novels are lacking so many of the essential elements needed to tell a strong, compelling, enduring story. The pillars of novel construction are weak, and some pillars are just missing altogether. If your novel does not have all twelve pillars constructed properly, your novel will collapse.

So we're going to be taking a long (and hopefully exciting) look at the roles secondary characters play in your novel—because those roles are really important.

They Must Serve a Purpose

All too often, as what happens with subplots, secondary characters are thrown into a novel without much thought or purpose. This is a bad thing. Just as with every element in your story, your secondary characters have to serve very specific purposes. They should be created each for a reason, to play a key part in the story.

Too often writers throw characters into their novel that they think are entertaining or will provide some drama or laughs, without giving thought to the bigger picture, hoping this will make it look as if a lot is happening, when actually all these characters do is clutter and distract from the main story.

Subplots that are just thrown in without thought do nothing to help give meaning and strength to the overall story, and the same is true with random secondary characters that are inserted for no clear reason. Everything you put in your novel should be done with deliberate purpose, and the type of secondary characters you create can make or break your story.

I will venture to say that much of the success of a great novel hinges on the secondary characters in the story.

So with that said, we're going to consider the types of characters you might have in your novel and the roles they play in relation to your protagonist. Because, all that matters regarding those characters is their relation to your main character and how they either help or hinder him from reaching his goal.

It's All about Who They Are

This isn't just about plot elements—what you have these characters *do*. It's more about who they *are*. About relationships. Sure, you will need these secondary characters to do things that advance the plot. But more importantly, these characters effect change in your main character. They play key roles in his character arc, while they themselves have strong character arcs.

Here's the key to creating strong, meaningful, complex characters in your novel: develop them just as deeply as you develop your main character. Give them a core need (preferably one that clashes with that of your protagonist) a big fear, and a lie they believe about themselves and the world.

This speaks to the heart of their motivation—in everything they do and say. In addition, all characters must not only have a past and history that has made them who they are in a believable way, they have to have a life outside the main plot.

Plot Layers for Secondary Characters

Yes, you want to create major and minor plots for these characters. There should be one major thing that a secondary character is concerned with, that is taking up most of her time and attention *apart from your protagonist*. And there can be some minor issues she is dealing with as well. Giving secondary characters those layers of plot that I spoke about will make them real, complex, and believable.

But . . . before you go there, you must first come up with some characters for you novel. And the way you do this is by focusing on your protagonist's core need, his plot goal for the book, and his inner motivation. There are specific roles each character plays in your story, and although there are no set rules as to how many characters you need to have, know that there are three basic types of secondary characters you will find in novels and movies, and we'll be examining these three types.

If you keep in mind, though, that every character in your novel needs to serve a purpose—to add richness to the story in more than just a visual way—you will be well on your way to building a strong pillar that will add support to your story.

Spend some time thinking about the characters you already have in your story, then take some time really delving into their core need, their greatest fear, and the lie they believe. Make sure these characteristics are created deliberately so that they can either clash with those needs and fears of your protagonist or provide the means for support and help.

The Cast of Characters in a Novel

Life is interesting when you have interesting people around you. But we shouldn't be writing novels just to showcase fascinating characters. Novels should be keenly focused, and those secondary characters, however colorful or intriguing, play a specific role.

If it's true (and I wholeheartedly believe it is) that the purpose of telling a story is to evoke emotion from your readers, what better way to do it than to show meaningful, purposeful relationships? The best novels, to me, are about characters who undergo significant change, and if you can create a character arc in your novel for your protagonist that has him change greatly and in meaningful ways by the end of the book, you are far along on the road to constructing a great novel.

What Facilitates Change?

You can have events bring about change in your protagonist (and in any or all of your secondary characters as well), and they should. Your plot should have waves of incidents that affect your character and get him to make hard choices, question his beliefs and attitudes, and rethink his decisions and goals.

But if you think about how and when you have been influenced the most to change a belief, behavior, attitude, or decision, you might agree that it was usually due to the influence of another person—usually a person with whom you had some sort of relationship. A stranger might suggest a course of action to you, and you might consider it. But if someone close to you—someone you care deeply for—urges you to reconsider your opinion or decision, that carries a lot more weight. If someone we love is passionate about something, they often *persuade* us to change.

It's All about Persuasion

My Speech instructor in college said that everything we belief, feel, buy, eat, wear, and read is due to someone persuading us. Whether directly or through advertising or some other means of communication, just about everything we do, buy, and "are" is the result of being persuaded. We are persuaded to try a new hairstyle, taste a new food, read a book by an unknown (to us) author, have Lasik surgery, buy a car, donate to a charity—all because someone, somehow, persuaded us.

Our goal as novelists is to persuade our readers—to get them to feel something in particular, to evoke emotion in them. The purpose of secondary characters, then, in a novel, is to also persuade. Their job is to persuade the protagonist in some way: to think or act differently, to see a situation in a new light, or to change some behavior or action. Whether they do this overtly, covertly, or even unconsciously depends upon the role and nature of the character in the story. But persuade they do.

When I say *persuade*, I mean it in the general sense of influencing behavior. An antagonist in a story won't necessarily stand around trying to convince the hero to do or not do something. He might, by his actions, *push* the hero in a direction. His opposition is persuasive in that he triggers a response in the hero that causes reaction.

Action-Reaction

If you keep in mind that the basic structure of storytelling is action-reaction, action-reaction, then secondary characters are in the story to persuade. To create "action" so that the protagonist can "react." That may seem simple, but it's the basic idea.

Since that's the case, you can see why having random, albeit colorful, characters populating your novel will not benefit you or serve the interests of your story unless they play key persuasive roles.

The Difference between Secondary and Minor Characters

Often you will have a cast of characters sprinkled through your scenes, each adding something to enhance the story. Sometimes those characters are just in the background, like extras in a movie. They are necessary, though, because you can't, for example, have a big cocktail party with only your hero and three secondary characters. People at that party, who have "bit parts" or maybe just a few seconds of "screen time," may add the texture and color needed to bring your scenes to life.

But those characters are fleeting and inconsequential. They're minor characters. In contrast, the essential secondary characters are ones you carefully develop, for they impact your plot and protagonist in big ways (even if those incidents appear to be minor). They should, as I mentioned earlier, have lives of their own. They should have a core need, a fear or two, a lie they believe about themselves and the world, and their needs and dreams and desires should clash with your protagonist's at times (some more than others, and some more often than others).

So let's take a look at the three basic types of characters in the supporting cast for your novel. You might have many secondary characters that play these roles, but there are three basic *types*— meaning, these characters serve a specific purpose in relation to your protagonist.

Chapter 18: The Three Basic Character Types in Your Story

As I've said repeatedly, novels are centered on a protagonist pursuing some visible goal, and this group of secondary characters appears in the novel to impact that in some way. But characters, just like real people, aren't always so simply defined in motive, purpose, or intent.

Some characters embody all three types at times. But if you find you don't have these types in your story, consider adding them. For, most of the great novels and movies have a strong supporting cast of characters. If we keep in mind that novels should be a reflection of real life, we will have a cast of characters that play the same kinds of roles as the people in our lives.

The Nemesis

I'm going to start with what might be considered the easiest or most obvious of secondary character types, but instead of thinking of a stereotyped "bad guy," which not all novels have or should have, think more in terms of anyone who stands in the way of the hero reaching his goal.

This means even an ally or friend—someone who thinks she has the hero's best interests at heart—can be a nemesis. Some call such a character an antagonist. I like that term because it reminds me of *antagonize* (for obvious reasons). Anyone who antagonizes or causes "agony" to your character can be an antagonist.

One character might wholly be opposed to your hero the whole novel through. Another might start off as an ally and switch camps, which is a very common plot structure. But a character that is in actuality an *ally* or friend would not be considered a "nemesis."

We all have moments in which we disagree with someone we love, or fight with him. Doesn't mean we're his enemy or opponent at heart. Likewise, an antagonist may not even realize she is one, but the reader does, and her role in the story makes her one. Needless to say, most antagonists in real life—and, one hopes, in novels too—really believe they are doing what's right and even best for the protagonist (however misguided we may feel they are).

An antagonist could be a real evil, mean character, or she could be an overly sweet and well-meaning elderly neighbor. There is no typical "face" for a nemesis. If you keep in mind the definition of this type of character—that she is in the story to stand in the way of the hero reaching his goal—you will see the potential for lots of different "faces" in your novel. There are few things worse in our lives than "well-meaning friends" who really want to . . . *persuade* us in a different direction. There's that word again—*persuade*.

If you think in terms of the antagonist hoping, trying, or wishing to persuade your hero away from the direction he is going in, you have an antagonist.

Motive Defines the Character Type

But . . . it's important to consider motive. Again, an ally or friend may try to persuade your hero to give up his goal—for some good reason. Maybe George's wife doesn't want him to risk his life on a dangerous search and rescue mission because she loves him and doesn't want to lose him. Well, in that moment, she is George's antagonist, standing in the way of his goal. But as a *character type*, she is an ally. Why? Because she wants him to succeed. She wants to help and support him. She has his best interests at heart. Yet, she is going to be an obstacle for him in the story if she is blocking his way.

Ah, you may be thinking, all this "character type" stuff is not so cut-and-dried. It's not. People are complex, fickle, selfish, self-sacrificing, and fearful. Depending on the situation and mind-set when something happens, each of us might react in an unpredictable way. One day we might love dogs and the next day hate them (after some mutt runs off with our lunch sack at the park). Because of a migraine, we might be mean and disagreeable to someone we love and to whom we have never said an unkind word previously.

Life is messy, difficult, stressful. Everyone reacts to stress differently and often inconsistently. You may want to make your role as writer easier by manufacturing consistent, predictable, stereotyped characters, but I would like to encourage you not to. Push yourself to create believable characters who are complex and sometimes unpredictable. If you can create a moment in your novel in which the hero and the antagonist agree on something and realize what they do have in common, you can have a powerful moment. Likewise, those moments in which the antagonist is actually vulnerable and/or empathetic can go a long way to making your story feel authentic.

Having one or more antagonists in your novel is so useful in many ways. By providing opposition, the hero can voice and demonstrate what he is passionate about, what he's willing to risk, and why he's after that goal. Nemesis characters provide the means to amplify and showcase the themes in your story, for they often take the opposing view.

Rethink the Stereotype

Why am I saying all this? Because the temptation, especially with the nemesis character, is to defer to stereotype. To make bad guys really bad to the point that they are comic-book cutouts, which is what I see nine times out of ten in the manuscripts I critique.

The best villains in literature, to me, are the ones you almost like (but would never admit it!) and find fascinating. They are usually complex, full of inner conflict, but have moments of grace or kindness that seem contradictory. Those moments, though, turn a predictable stereotype into a riveting, believable nemesis.

So, I hope this all gets you thinking about the antagonist character types you may have in your novel. Whether you have one specific nemesis for your protagonist or have multiple characters that play that role, the nemesis character does not want your hero to reach his goal. He himself should have needs, fears, and goals he is striving for based on what he believes. He may be evil, greedy, psychotic, or a sociopath. Or he might instead be a friend who is fearful of losing something precious to him, and who believes with all his heart the protagonist must not reach his goal. It depends on your story.

If you don't have anyone opposing your protagonist, spend some time thinking how to create someone. Make his needs and goals clash with your hero's. Make him believe he is right and has the right to his belief. Great novels are all about tension and conflict, and without opposition to the protagonist, you won't have a story worth telling.

Secondary Characters Should Change and Grow

When we looked at the nemesis type, I cautioned about slipping into stereotype, which is a real problem with this kind of character. But this is also a danger for the other secondary character types in your novel. So I am going to tell you what I think is the key to creating genuine secondary characters: showing them changing and growing along with your protagonist.

That doesn't mean they change in the same way—not at all. Every character should have his or her own goal and character arc. But characters who never change or grow at all through a novel are kind of like Mary Poppins: "practically perfect in every way." A perfect antagonist, friend, ally, or romance character who starts off with a particular attitude, personality, or mind-set and who never changes at all or never has one moment of self-doubt or contradiction or reversal in thought or behavior isn't all that believable.

I've said this before: people are complex, messy, contradictory, hypocritical, unpredictable. We humans are like the sea that tosses and churns. Well, maybe you know some people who are as steady as the rock of Gibraltar. At least they appear to be. Are they interesting though? Probably not. Only when they do something completely unexpected, even shocking, do they snag our interest.

Same for characters. Make them stagnant, and watch the reader's eyes droop and the snores start to slip out of her mouth . . .

So, with that reminder, let's look at the next secondary character type found in a novel: the ally or reflection character.

Your Protagonist Needs an Ally

You'll often see in movies or novels one main ally character. This is a character introduced early, usually at the outset of the story. Her role is clear—she's there to support the hero, and stands by and helps as the hero pursues his goal. She may or may not also be a romance character, but often she is a friend who shares thoughts and feelings, gives advice, and may often be in conflict with the protagonist.

As in real life, we have allies—friends who are there for us. Some of us are blessed with terrific friends who will drop anything to come to our aid. And the best friends will call us out on our stuff if we are in the wrong or headed down a bad path.

I remember when this slogan came out years ago: "Friends don't let friends drive drunk." That about sums up the sentiment. A good friend is a treasure, and if you can create at least one true ally character in your novel to stand by your protagonist, you will help raise your novel a notch in the realm of believability.

Like a Mirror

An ally character is sometimes called a "reflection." I like this term because the best kind of friend will reflect back to you who you are. These friends act as mirrors, and often when you can't see yourself clearly (metaphorically speaking), they can and do reflect back to you what and how you really are. This role or behavior for a secondary character can be a great element in your novel in key places.

There are doors your protagonist must go through, hard choices he has to make. He might slip back, have fear and doubt, second-guess himself. Here's where the reflection character comes in—to show the protagonist why and maybe how he can make it through the door. A romance character, too, often has the role of believing in the hero when he doesn't believe in himself. Giving him the push needed to keep going.

We all wish we had true friends like that. And so, giving your hero a true friend who can help him reach his goal is a great type of character to have in your story. But here's my caveat again: that character shouldn't be in your novel just to say the right words at the right time, every time. Don't make her "practically perfect" Mary Poppins. Give her her own core need, fear, lie, and goal. Give her a secondary plot that clashes with your protagonist's.

Yes, Even Allies Should Clash

Consider your theme, and come up with a problem that secondary character has that will set her on the opposite side of the "issue" from your protagonist. Let them clash at key moments. That's real life. You might even have your secondary character be so angry she turns her back on your hero (or vice versa). In "the dark night of the soul" moment before the climax, if you can make your hero lose everything he loves and have his entire support system (his allies) abandon him, that's a good thing. The more you can make the attaining of his goal seem hopeless, the better. And one great way to aid in creating that darkest moment is to have his closest friend turn on him or leave him because of something said or done by the protagonist (or so presumed. Having misdirection or misunderstanding is a great element to consider adding). Yes, to be a great novelist, you do need to be a sadist.

Remember, the key to creating great secondary characters is to show them changing and growing. Their interaction with the protagonist—the conflict, arguments, and pain they suffer in dealing with the main character—should create change in attitude and behavior. By the end of the book, the more you can have your ally character(s) now seeing life differently, feeling closer to your hero, and having more understanding of and compassion for your hero, the better.

So don't just throw an ally or two into your novel as filler. Spend time crafting each character carefully. Give your allies rich, complex, unique personalities, background, and voices. Give them needs that clash with your hero's. But make them loyal, even if they slip for a moment. They need to be there for your hero, stick by him, speak truth in love, reflect back what the hero needs to see in order to understand and move one step closer to his goal. Whether your ally is comedic relief, a serious therapist, or a nagging mother, that character has the hero's bests interests at heart; she means to help him reach his goal.

Donald Maass wrote in *Writing 21st Century Fiction*: "The more unlike anyone else you make a character, the more universal that character will become." He says that's counterintuitive, and it is, right? But I agree with his assessment. We want our characters to be universal so everyone can relate to them. But stereotyping them is not the way. Originality is. Infuse each secondary character—the nemesis, the ally, and the romance character—all with originality, and your novel will stand out. Your pillar of support will be strong.

Did I mention romance? Yep, that's the third character type in novels, so let's explore it.

Bring a Bit of Romance to Your Novel

Wait, you don't have any romance in your novel? There's no law that says you must. But before you shake your head and refuse to consider the possibility, think about this . . .

131

It's perfectly fine if you do not have a romance element in your novel. Your genre may not call for one, nor your premise or story line. And that's acceptable. You aren't often going to see a romance thread in a children's book, for example. However, if you're writing about teens or adults (or even mature aliens, robots, or animals), you might consider putting one in.

Why? Because most readers (okay, I'll venture to assume this) enjoy a bit of romance or even romantic entanglement. Why? Because it reflects real life. Most people's lives have some romance in them (or they wish they did). Most people like to see some romantic exchange in a novel. Romance, being (often) a big part of real life means it usually has a place in a novel.

Romance Is Part of Real Life

A character that has no interest at all in romance or love or some sort of intimate relationship may seem lacking. A character who, at some point in her life, hasn't suffered a bad relationship, breakup, betrayal, or hurt over love hardly seems human. So even if your protagonist isn't involved or looking for love at the moment, giving her a history of some romantic relationship will make her more real. And what she experienced (or suffered) in that relationship should help shape both her character and how she looks at the opposite sex.

Again, the premise and genre determine this. Many novels have no place for romance or a romance thread. But I will daresay that a lot of novels are missing this element and could really use it. And it doesn't have to be a current romance happening now in the story. Often a writer has created a protagonist—let's say, a male—who seems to never have been in love, or had a girlfriend, or dated, or was married at some point, or even thought about the opposite sex (if that's his bent). Most people would say, yeah, that really isn't normal. As he goes after his goal, whatever it is, he seems to be clueless there are attractive women out there. He never thinks about them or seems to ever want to get into a romantic relationship on any level. He never notices if a woman is attractive or not. He hardly seems human.

Now, maybe you want a character like that—someone dysfunctional, sheltered, messed-up. But that's a very specific, deliberate character aspect. What I see a lot is a lack of "normal" with a lot of characters. Yes, they have a core need and a goal they are pursuing in the novel, but somehow they are missing this whole part of their nature and life.

The Romance Character's Purpose

Now, with that said, the inclusion of an actual romance character type in the story is a different matter than just showing a guy flirting with some gals in various scenes. The role of a romance character is usually fairly specific. When it comes to the character's inner motivation, the romance character is usually the one who understands the hero, sees him for who he truly is, and believes in him (maybe even when he doesn't believe in himself). As screenwriting instructor Michael Hauge teaches: the romance character sees the hero's true essence, what his potential is, who he can (and will) become at the end of the story. While the hero is putting on a face or persona for the world to see in order to protect his heart and avoid vulnerability, the romance character sees past that persona. That is one essential role of the romance character.

The romance character in most successful stories is not someone who is already on the scene in a relationship with the hero (and although I've been defaulting mostly to male hero/female romantic interest, the reverse is equally valid in all I've been discussing). She is someone who *grows into the role* of the romantic interest. Often the hero "gets the girl" as a kind of reward or compensation for reaching his goal. Why? Because by the end of the movie or novel, the hero has come into his essence, proven himself (sometimes more to himself than for her benefit), is now ready for that commitment, whereas up until the end he may not have been.

A great example of this that popped into my mind is the movie *Groundhog Day*. Not your typical romance story. In fact, throughout the movie viewers are given very little indication this is intended to be a romance story. Sure—obnoxious, self-absorbed, and tactless weatherman Phil Connors has the hots for his segment producer, Rita—who looks upon him with utter disdain, and rightly so. But the premise of this movie isn't centered on his winning the girl. Phil is stuck in repeating this awful one day in Punxsutawney, Pennsylvania, on Groundhog's Day because he has to learn certain things in life. And one of the things he learns is that for anyone to really love him—and for him to be able to truly love another—he has to change and become a compassionate, selfless, and caring individual. All the hard knocks he

suffers lead him to becoming a worthy, good man, and as his reward—
when he finally stops striving after the girl—he gets her . . . and
deserves her.

An Ally or a Reflection Character

The romance type can also be an ally or reflection character. She
doesn't always fit that role, but it's common to see. In addition, the
romance character can become an antagonist, and often does. Or starts
as an antagonist and becomes the romantic interest (as we see in
Groundhog Day). So this character type has a lot of flexibility. Just keep
in mind that a true romance character type is defined by the hero's
motivation and is part of the hero's visible goal—he wants to get the
girl. The pursuit of her love is tied in with his overarching larger goal
for the novel (unless you are writing strictly romance, in which, in some
cases, getting the girl is everything).

So now that we've covered these three basic secondary character
types, I'm going to share the secret to crafting genuine characters for
your novel.

Chapter 19: The Secret to Crafting Genuine Characters for Your Novel

Think about what makes you interested or drawn to certain people. What qualities of theirs pull you in? Is it a sense of humor? Some interesting hobby or skill? Engaging style of talking or fascinating facial expressions or gestures?

Every person in your novel should have something about him that makes him interesting. It takes some work to create original, fresh, unpredictable characters, but it's worthwhile to do. If you don't want to spend an evening at a party among boring people, how can you expect your readers to be willing to spend ten to twenty hours of their life "hanging out" with your boring characters? We owe it to our readers to take the time to give them a unique cast of characters.

Real People Are Wholly Individual

Real people are influenced by their upbringing. Depending on their socioeconomic environment, ethnicity and subculture, geographic roots, education, and many other factors, people will not only vary in the way they move, think, and talk, they will acquire individual mannerisms and quirks and habits.

Listen to people sometime at a coffee shop or a park. Give yourself the assignment to notice these little individual flairs that seem to define each person's personality. Be creative and imagine a history and present profile for each person as they walk by the park bench you are sitting on. Pay attention. Notice what stands out.

Word Whiskers

I love to give each of my characters a word whisker or two. What is a word whisker? It's an expression or phrase, or maybe even one word, that they repeat a lot (sometimes to the point of annoyance). Frank Zappa wrote a great song years back that his daughter "starred in" called "Valley Girl." I especially related to that song because, yes, I was a valley girl. I grew up in the San Fernando Valley in Los Angeles, and, like the "character" in his song, I hung out at the Galleria, and I did on occasion say "fer sure." In the song, among other word whiskers like "you know" and "gag me with a spoon," the singer repeated over and over: "fer sure, fer sure." The chorus of the song went: "She's a valley girl, fer sure, fer sure. She's a valley girl, and there ain't no cure."

Teenage girls in the "valley" decades ago (when I was young) talked like that. Yes, it was annoying and oftentimes obnoxious, and who knows where all these expressions actually came from (who cares)? But I hope you get my point. Memorable characters often have a unique way of talking, and say some repeated phrases they've glomped on to. It may seem like a small thing, but it's the small quirks and behaviors we have that make us unique (and, we hope, interesting) people.

Characters in *The Closer*

You can make annoying, boring, insipid characters you need to have in your story interesting by giving them quirks and weird hobbies and strange gestures. I love the TV series *The Closer*. It's not just a great show because of the screenwriting, which is wonderful, or the terrific episode plots. What makes *The Closer* so terrific is the characters that populate the series. The main character, played by Kira Sedgewick, is a Southern gal who comes to LA to be the head homicide detective in a precinct. Immediately she clashes with everyone there because of her quirks, foibles, upbringing, manners, perspective—and list goes on.

In addition to her being so completely at odds with everyone on her team (who all have to obey her and who instantly dislike her), she has really funny, unique quirks. First off, she has absolutely no sense of direction and gets lost at every turn (which her disgruntled subordinates take advantage of in the way of practical jokes). Next, she is obsessed with sweets and hides them everywhere, indulging in them with great guilt, which makes you wonder why she's so neurotic about that. Then, this tough detective is absolutely terrorized by her sweet Southern parents. She lapses into an intimidated little girl when she has to answer to "Daddy." All these crazy characteristics make her highly entertaining.

The more each character is set in his or her way and has strong personality traits, the more they will all clash with one another, which is what is desired. The creators of *The Closer* populated the investigative team with a riot of wild characters that are wholly believable, each with his own set of odd behaviors, speech, and attitudes. I highly recommend you watch a couple of seasons of this show (even if you aren't into cop shows) just to study the characters.

The brilliance of this show is revealed in the way these characters grow, change, and develop over the seasons. I mentioned in the last chapter how critical it is to have secondary characters grow and change alongside the protagonist. In *The* Closer, as the main character adjusts to life in LA and proves her worth to her team, those who at first opposed her become her most loyal supporters. By putting them through crucibles of fire together, they grow and change together, and their relationships strengthen.

And this is the best thing you can do to create genuine characters for your novel—have them go through tough times together. Have them deal with each other at their best and their worst, but know that conflict is the crucible that will put those relationships through severe testing.

An Exercise to Help You

Here's a simple exercise you can do. Make a list of your secondary characters—all of them. Even the minor characters, like that waitress who shows up a few times in scenes at the diner. Hopefully you have already created a strong background for these characters so they each have a specific upbringing that influences who they are. You've come up with their core needs, deepest dreams, greatest fears—all designed to serve the needs of the plot and create conflict with your protagonist (yes, even the allies and romance character types).

Now, give each one a physical quirk or behavior that fits her personality. Maybe the waitress clicks her pen repeatedly; that's her nervous habit. Or she might bite her nails because she is wired on too much coffee.

Give each character a phrase or two, maybe a saying, he likes to spout. Don't get corny here, but again, if you listen to people talk at the park or Starbuck's, you will pick up on these word whiskers. Don't clutter your novel with "ums" and "uhs" to mimic real life. Those aren't interesting word whiskers. Instead, think of something catchy.

In my fantasy novel *The Wolf of Tebron*, I created a wolf that embodies some of the wisdom of G. K. Chesterton, a writer I feel had gobs of great sayings (I also drew from C. S. Lewis). So I gave my wolf, Ruyah, two things he said over and over: "Fancy that," and "It is said among wolves . . ." My protagonist got a bit tired of hearing him say those words so often, but having Ruyah do so fit his character and, I hope, made him memorable. I recall a minor character in the TV series *LA Law* decades ago—an annoying guy who always said "Correct me if I'm wrong." He was a great character, and I wanted to whack him upside the head all the time. But that phrase of his was almost iconic for his personality—perfect.

Don't overdo it here. Don't fill your novel with crazy characters all spouting repeated silly expressions to excess. Some people don't have favorite phrases. But they will have some gesture or facial expression or quirk that is unique to them, and that's what you want to bring out in a way that showcases who they are.

You Should Create Characters You Love

Try to create characters you love (or love to hate). That entertain, move, or inspire you. If you can get your characters to make you laugh or cry, you are on the path to creating a memorable novel.

So what's the secret to crafting genuine characters? Don't settle for the stereotype. Spend time really observing people and notice their individual mannerisms, way of speaking, gestures. Great characters are wholly unique, have odd quirks, say repeated words and phrases they've picked up. When each character you create fascinates *you* to the point that you want to be around them and see what they do and say next, you've done your job.

If we want to write great stories, we need to populate them with great characters. And that means breaking free of stereotypes and going for originality. It takes work, but it's worth it.

This wraps up our exploration into the sixth key pillar of novel construction: Secondary Characters with Their Own Needs. I hope you've learned some great insights into how to craft these important characters for your novel.

And now . . . you get a new checklist! Be sure to carefully consider all the twelve sets of questions. Photocopy the checklist or type this link into your Internet browser: http://bit.ly/1zB1OC2.

If you can answer these questions to your satisfaction, you know you have a strong pillar. Ready for the next one? We'll be looking at another of my favorites: Setting with a Purpose.

Inspection Checklist #6
Secondary Characters with their Own Needs

Question #1:

Do you have at least three supporting characters (SCs) that play key roles and are there to either help or hinder your protagonist? List how they do this in the story.

Question #2:

List three main SCs. List each of their core needs, goals, greatest fear, deepest desire. How do these create conflict or support for your protagonist?

Question #3:

Can you think of a key scene to put in your novel in which your most supportive SC opposes your protagonist regarding her goal? Put it in.

Question #4:

Who is the primary reflection character/ally for your protagonist? What key moment is in your novel that showcases his support?

Question #5:

Who is the primary antagonist in your novel? What key moment showcases the big conflict and issue between them?

Question #6:

What are three ways or moments in which you show your antagonist(s) as human, vulnerable, almost sympathetic?

Question #7:

In what big way do your SCs create Conflict with High Stakes for your protagonist? Can you make the conflict and stakes bigger?

Question #8:

What is the big moment in which the most supportive SC helps the protagonist change and/or reach her visible goal in or right before the climax?

Question #9:

What A and B plots and subplots have you developed for each of your main SCs? How do they help/hinder the protagonist's goal?

Question #10:

In what ways do you use the SCs to bring out the themes in your novel? Can you come up with at least three key scenes?

Question #11:

Do you have a romance character and element in your novel? Summarize 6-12 scenes (1 line) that show how the relationship gradually develops with conflict and connection.

Question #12:

How does the romance character act as a reflection for your protagonist? Lists three key moments when he/she helps the protagonist see his/her true self.

Pillar #7: Setting with a Purpose

Chapter 20: Evoking Powerful, Meaningful Settings

Sad but true, setting and locale in novels is mostly ignored. It's as if writers feel they must sacrifice attention to setting on the altar of getting the story moving, but nothing could be further from the truth.

Setting serves a number of very powerful, key functions in a novel's scenes, and that's why it's an essential pillar of novel construction. Without setting, how can you have a story? Some (many) scenes I've edited and critiqued appear to be taking place in the void of space or some nebulous location. The writer seems so intent on conveying dialog or explaining about the characters that he forgets (or thinks it is unimportant) to mention where his characters just happen to be.

And then there are other manuscripts in which setting is occasionally mentioned in passing, but almost as an afterthought, as if the writer knows he should say something about where his characters are but feels it is so unimportant, he just throws out a few token lines that objectively name the place or sketch a vague description and moves on.

And that's a shame, because a writer like that is missing out on a great opportunity to bring his novel to life. The more real a place is to readers, the easier they can be transported there to experience the story.

Try to Be Original and Purposeful

Too often setting is relegated to restaurants, with characters sitting around eating or drinking. Some novels I've critiqued have more than twenty restaurant scenes. Unless you are doing *My Dinner with Andre*, stay away from scenes like that unless that is the *best* place for your character to be for that scene. It's not just the repetition that makes those scenes boring, it's the fact that characters are merely sitting and talking—not doing anything all that interesting. Try to be original, imaginative.

First consideration is the *overall locale* of your novel's setting, which may be one place, like a small town, or have an international hodgepodge of locales, such as in Ludlum's Bourne series. It may be that your premise requires a very specific location, but if not, take the time to think about your concept and the protagonist's goal, and consider places to set your characters in that can provide as much interest, potential for conflict, and utility for your story. And of course it has to be a place that works for your protagonist's background and personality.

Next consideration is *the individual scenes* in your book. If you are trying to show a character's well-rounded life, you will want a number of different locales showcasing his job, his family, his hobbies, where he hangs out with his friends. But the trap for many writers is when they choose random settings for no apparent reason as a backdrop for the story. Or default to the same setting over and over. And that means missing out on a very useful structural components for a story. Setting is so powerful in our lives, and it can—and should—be in the lives of our characters.

Build Your World

You may feel that if you are not writing a fantasy novel, you don't have to "build your world." But you do. You might ask, why would you need to "build" New York City, for example, when most people know a lot about that city from TV, movies, news, and even personal experience?

The answer circles back again to the point that your novel is shown through the eyes of the POV characters. This means that in every scene, someone is experiencing the place they are in as the plot develops. New York, to you, is going to feel different and mean different things than it is to me. And that locale may mean different things to you at various times in your life, depending upon what you are going through or have gone through. New York, to each of your characters situated there, is going to be experienced differently.

The more you can have the setting of each scene affect and impact your characters in some way, the more real and personal your story will feel. If setting isn't all that important to your concept and plot, spend some time thinking about how to make it so. Consider changing the locale your novel takes place in to one with greater purpose for your story.

Why not go through your scenes and list all the places you show your characters? Are they purposeful? Do they set the right mood for the scene? Do they evoke memories or feelings in your POV character?

How Settings and Locale Shape Us and the Characters We Create

Consider for a moment how locale has shaped you. Where did you grow up? What memories do you have from when you were a kid and cruised around your neighborhood?

I can picture just about every house for miles around my childhood suburban Los Angeles neighborhood because I rode my bike all the time, up and down the hills of Sherman Oaks, California, south of "The Boulevard," as it was called. I have fond memories of the local park with its huge community pool, where I swam on hot summer days. I can smell the salty air mixed with coconut oil at Santa Monica beach, and see the sweltering heat waves coming up off the hot parking lot, and hear the squawking of seagulls fighting over fish guts on the smelly pier. I can taste the chewy, hot, greasy fried clams and hear the music wafting from the carousel and feel my sticky swimsuit full of sand, making me itchy in the backseat of our big old car as we drove the freeways home, sleepy after a long day at the beach.

I spent my early childhood summers in the Bronx, New York, in my grandparents' hot (no A/C) apartment, with mosquitoes attacking me at night while I hid under itchy wool blankets. I attended PS 93 (the local elementary school) for a few months, where I was teased for my California accent. I was terrified to take the trash down to the basement, which was smelly and dark and where I imagined evil men or monsters lurked. I experienced many uncomfortable, unpleasant, tense, and fearful moments as a child in New York; I didn't go back for

144

more than forty years because of the distaste I had for that place. But when I did finally return, I was surprised at how much I enjoyed it.

Past Is Present

We can all get lost in specific locales that are rich in sensory details. So why do most writers tend to ignore setting? Setting forms us and contributes to who we are. The choices we make as adults as to where we will live and work and play are influenced by our past experiences with setting. Setting is highly influential to us and should also be such for your characters, so I am hoping in these chapters to get you to consider Setting with a Purpose as a strong and essential pillar of novel support.

If you take the time when creating your characters to think about setting as an important part of their background, you will create richer characters. Don't just give your characters a general past. Know exactly where they grew up and what that place (or places) was like and how it affected them.

Try coming up with at least three events that happened to them growing up that tied in with the setting and that affected them for life. For example, if you have a character who grew up on a rugged coast and who watched his fisherman father die in a storm at sea, he will have some very intense conflicted feelings about spending a day on a friend's sailboat. And if you add a storm to that present-day outing, think how that might affect him.

You don't have to create some tragedy in a character's past that is tied to setting (although that can often be great to do depending on your plot), but at very least, think how region and locale greatly influence your characters and find ways to bring that into your story. If you've seen the movie and/or TV miniseries *Fargo*, there's a great example of setting influencing attitude, speech/vernacular, and character. The setting steals the show.

We all have pasts, but too many writers create characters that have none. They show up in novels as ciphers, appearing on the stage with no background whatsoever, and as a result hardly have any personality. Too often I read novels with flat, boring, nothing characters. And a large reason they are that way is they have no connection to locale— past or present.

Draw from Your Own Connections to Setting

Think of the three most important settings or locations in your past, where something very important or intense happened to you. This may take some time—or not. Where did you meet your spouse? What is the best or worst trip you ever took in your life? What is the worst tragedy you witnessed or suffered and where were you? Do you feel creeped out when you walk through the corridors of a hospital? If you're an ER nurse, maybe not. But if you watched someone you love die in a hospital bed, you might feel uneasy.

We want to make our characters feel. I would say *feel strongly*. The more your characters can emote in believable, intense ways, the more chance your readers will be moved and affected as well. If you deliberately place your character in a setting that will bring up strong emotions in him, you will have a better, more effective scene than one in which you place your character in the local Starbuck's just because you haven't bothered to consider coming up with a more appropriate setting.

How to Choose Setting with a Purpose

Keep in mind this main point: the setting should be determined by the high point of the scene. Stop and think what main plot point or character insight you are going to reveal in a scene.

It may be you have no real choice as to where to set some scenes; they have to take place in certain locations. But if you are going to have a high moment of reveal or conflict, consider some choices of locale that will be compelling, interesting, provide variety, and most importantly be significant or emotive for your characters. Think about the key moments in your novel when your character has the greatest insights, pain, confrontation, or despair. If you can set those scenes in places that have emotional impact on your character, the scene will be stronger.

For example, you may have a scene planned that shows your main character having a fight with her boyfriend over her unwanted pregnancy. You *could* have the argument in a restaurant. Fine. But what if you have the argument in front of a preschool daycare or a hospital nursery ward, where she is visiting a friend who just had a baby? What if this character is conflicted about aborting, and all around her are cute laughing toddlers? Or screeching babies needing to be fed and changed

146

and cared for? Depending on your plot and character arcs, these settings could add to the tension and hit home the high moment of your scene in a more powerful way.

Just as setting has shaped who you are, let setting shape your characters and influence them in the scenes they are in. Create setting with a purpose.

Showing Settings through the Eyes of Your Characters

"It is impossible to powerfully capture a place via objective description—at least to capture it in a way that readers will not skim. Only through the eyes and heart of a character does place come truly alive" (Donald Maass, *The Fire in Fiction*).

You may not have thought about setting in this way, but it's all about the POV character. Each person reacts differently to a specific setting. If you and a group of your friends were transported to someplace you'd never been, you would each notice, like, dislike, and be curious about different things.

All too often writers take a brief moment in some scenes (though not all) to describe the setting in a very dull, descriptive way. But just as they may do with some characters (noting superficial things like clothing, eye color, and hairstyle), they often give a broad and boring sweep of a setting, if at all. More often than not, there is no description of setting, and if I could be paid a nickel for every scene I've critiqued that does not show the setting, I would be wealthy indeed.

General and Specific Settings

There are two specifics to consider about setting. The first is the setting of the whole novel itself, which I touched on earlier. The premise and plot will determine much of the setting *in general*, but often there is leeway to be creative with specific places. Whether your story is set in a small Southern town, or in a sprawling city, or a fantasy world, within that locale are many different places you can stage your scenes.

I'm not sure why writers tend to default to placing their characters in coffee shops and restaurants so often. Yes, we tend to go to those places, but think about how many hours a week you are actually in a restaurant or coffee shop. And then think about how interesting a milieu such a place normally is. Do you really get excited to go to Starbuck's to get an espresso? (I mean, aside from longing for that drink.) Do you expect exciting things to happen there? Not likely, although I have seen some pretty wild and inspiring people come through some coffee shop doors in the many hours I have spent writing in these places.

But I hope you see my point. Since your novel is primarily about one character and the changes and challenges she goes through to reach a goal she is passionate about, the more selective and deliberate you are about choosing setting, the better your story could be. And so many places could be great stages upon which your character and plot arcs play out.

Setting Is a Matter of POV

Take a look at this brief passage from the Pulitzer Prize–winning novel *The Goldfinch* by Donna Tartt. Her young protagonist, Theo, is thirteen, and he lives in New York City. The inciting incident in the novel's early pages shows Theo in a tragic, horrific explosion in which he loses his mother. Notice how Tartt connects Theo's setting to his emotional state—something she does on every single page of her novel.

It was just the kind of shop my mother would have liked— packed tightly, a bit dilapidated, with stacks of old books on the floor. But the gates were pulled down and the place was closed.

Most of the stores didn't open until noon, or one. To kill some time I walked over to Greenwich Avenue, to the Elephant and Castle, a restaurant where my mother and I ate sometimes when we were downtown. But the instant I stepped in, I realized my mistake. The mismatched china elephants, even the ponytailed waitress in a black T-shirt who approached me, smiling: it was too overwhelming, I could see the corner table where my mother and I had eaten lunch the last time we were there, I had to mumble an excuse and back out the door.

I stood on the sidewalk, heart pounding. Pigeons flew low in the sooty sky. Greenwich Avenue was almost empty: a bleary male couple who looked like they'd been up fighting all night; a rumple-haired woman in a too-big turtleneck sweater, walking a dachshund toward Sixth Avenue. It was a little weird being in the Village on my own because it wasn't a place where you saw many kids on the street on a weekend morning; it felt adult, sophisticated, slightly alcoholic. Everybody looked hung over or as if they had just rolled out of bed.

Every inch of every street and building and room is seen through an emotional filter over Theo's eyes—all of it changed as he now faces life without his mother. Setting comes alive on every page of *The Goldfinch*.

I recently had the pleasure of listening to mystery writer Elizabeth George speak for an hour on setting, which is of great importance to her in her Inspector Lynley novels set in England. Although she is American, she spends much time traveling around the UK countryside finding general and specific settings for her novels. When she does so, she already has her basic plot and characters in mind, and she often knows specific scenes and their moments of reveal. So she looks for places in which, for example, a dead body might be dumped, or a location that features hiking trails over foggy moors where a murder might go unnoticed. While characters are truly at the heart of all her novels, she well knows that setting plays a huge role in shaping, defining, and influencing characters.

Take a look at this brief passage in *Playing for the Ashes* that follows one of her main characters in her series—Detective Sergeant Barbara Havers:

> Even before she'd acquired it, her tiny cottage had long been a symbol to Barbara. It meant liberation from a life that had held her chained for years to duty and ailing parents. But while making the move had given her the freedom from responsibility that she had dreamed of having, that same freedom brought a solitude that closed in on her at moments when she was least prepared to encounter it. So Barbara had taken a distinct if sardonic pleasure in the discovery that there were two means of getting to work each morning, both of them teeming with teeth-grating, ulcer-causing, and—best of all—loneliness-displacing distractions.
>
> She could fight the traffic in her ageing Mini, battling her way down Camden High Street to Mornington Crescent, where she could choose at least three different routes, all of which wound through the sort of life-in-a-medieval-city congestion that every day seemed to become more hopes of remedy. Or she could take the underground, which meant sinking into the bowels of Chalk Farm Station and waiting for a train with ever-decreasing hope

among the faithful but understandably irascible riders of the capricious Northern Line. And even then, not just any train would do, but one that passed through Embankment Station, where she could catch yet another train to St. James's Park.

It was a situation based firmly in the realm of cliché: On a daily basis, Barbara could choose between the devil and the deep blue sea.

. . . She endured the irritants with resignation. Another bloody commute. Another chance to conclude conveniently that her loneliness was really of no account because there was neither time nor energy at the end of the day for social interaction anyway.

George makes it very clear how Havers feels about her life by the way she deals with her commute to work—to her setting—which informs and reveals her character.

In my book *Shoot Your Novel*, I share a wonderful passage showcasing an establishing (opening) shot by John Le Carré in *The Constant Gardener*. It's such a great example of showing setting from a character's POV, I'm going to share it here.

Le Carré does a terrific job of using appropriate adjectives and his choice of words to reflect his POV character's mind-set. His protagonist, Justin Quayle, is on a dangerous journey trying to discover the details of his wife's death, which he suspects will turn out to be a murder. It's clear every word was chosen carefully. If you think writing a paragraph or two introducing the setting and time of your scene can only be boring, think again.

The mountain stood black against the darkening sky, and the sky was a mess of racing cloud, perverse island winds and February rain. The snake road was strewn with pebbles and red mud from the sodden hillside. Sometimes it became a tunnel of overhanging pine branches and sometimes it was a precipice with a free fall to the steaming Mediterranean a thousand feet below. He would make a turn and for no reason the sea would rise in a wall in front of him, only to fall back into the abyss as he made another. But no matter how many times he turned, the rain came straight at him, and when it struck the windscreen he felt the jeep wince under him like an old horse no longer fit for heavy pulling.

Look at some of the words he uses: *black, darkening* (his quest to find answers is getting that way), *perverse* (that too), *winds, rain, snake, sodden, tunnel, precipice* . . . I don't need to go on—you get the point. The reader has been watching Justin Quayle going through a similar emotional roller coaster, rising and falling into an abyss, turning one way then another, but getting nowhere fast. His task to find answers feels like he's prodding "an old horse no longer fit for heavy pulling." And the weight he is carrying is heavy. Powerful, right?

This is, to me, a perfect example of showing setting through the eyes, mood, mind-set, and heart of the character and *how he feels at that moment in the story*. Le Carré could have shown Quayle driving along a flat, boring highway on a sunny day, but that would have been a shame, wouldn't it? A waste of *opportunity to add texture and depth to the story*.

So don't waste valuable real estate in your novel by writing boring descriptions of setting just to "get it over with" and move on to the rest of the story. Start thinking about setting as essential—to your protagonist. Create a rich history for all your main characters that are linked to places in their past based on their core need and function in your novel. Do this, and you'll have a strong pillar of novel construction.

Chapter 21: Connecting Your Characters to Settings in Your Novel

We spend a lot of our time at work and home, and occasionally at restaurants and coffee shops, and that is ordinary life. And while we want to show our characters in *their* ordinary lives (at least sometimes), readers don't want "boring."

So the challenge for novelists is to come up with settings that are interesting. But settings are nothing by themselves; they must be experienced by the characters in your story, as Donald Maass noted. And the more you can create emotional connection to setting for those characters, the more alive the places will become. We looked at a few examples in novels that showed the POV character intrinsically tied with his or her setting. But how can you come up with emotionally charged settings for your characters?

Settings That Trigger Emotion

I had you think about places in your past that are emotionally charged to you. By thinking about specific places that have emotional triggers, it may help you come up with such places for your characters. I call those places "connected settings"—settings we connect strongly to emotionally.

Does your protagonist, for example, have a strong emotional connection to one or both parents (who may still be living or have died before your story starts)? By having your character visit a place that holds powerful memories of that parent, either positive or negative or both, those emotions can drive a scene, and the memories triggered there can induce conflict.

Let's say your protagonist has just had a huge fight with her mother over the man she plans to marry. She might drive back to her childhood home, or just go sit in the bedroom in her parents' house in which she spent her childhood. There, she might remember the vicious fights her parents had before they divorced and how painful they were to listen to. She might, at that moment, feel a strong determination to never be like her mother. Or, she may suddenly be afraid to commit to marriage, fearing her marriage may end up just like her parents'.

Conflict, Conflict, Conflict!

The place she is in can be a great tool to increasing her inner conflict, which is what you want. Inner conflict emotionally drives the character toward her visible goal in your story, so anything that can "stir up the waters" is going to be worthwhile. If she instead goes to Starbuck's after having a fight with her mother, she may just order her Americano coffee, blow it off, and get on with her day—and not have the intense emotions to mull through that a "connected" setting would have on her.

The most powerful scene to me in the movie *Minority Report* is the one in which the protagonist, John Anderton (played by Tom Cruise), takes the female Pre-Cog, Agatha, to his previous home, which his ex-wife, Lara, still lives in. They broke up years ago because their son was kidnapped and presumed murdered, and they couldn't bear the loss. Now, they hardly speak to or see each other, but John needs a temporary refuge for Agatha in order to solve a crime.

Lara and John end up in their son's room, and for a brief moment, it's as if the fast-action plot comes to a screeching halt in a moment of incredible poignancy. This scene is the very heart of the movie. It's a highly unexpected moment—for the viewer and the estranged couple. For Agatha stops them in their tracks by saying, "There is so much love in this house." She then "sees" the future their dead son would have had, recounting, "He's ten years old . . . he's surrounded by animals. He wants to be a vet . . . he's in high school. He likes to run. Like his father. . . . he's twenty-three and in love . . ." And on and on she goes, seeing this future that could have been.

And although what Lara and John hear breaks their hearts, it somehow breaks through their pain, so that by the end of the movie they get back together and Lara's pregnant (but not until a lot of suspenseful minutes pass on the screen!). That scene, that moment, so

153

powerful due to the characters' *emotional connection to setting*, is paramount in John's character arc. It is *the* scene that propels him to the place of needed healing. Without it, he would never get there. He would wallow in misery forever.

Key Moments in Your Story Need Key Settings

Could any other setting have had such a powerful effect on the characters or viewers? What could be more painful than sitting in your dead child's bedroom, amid all those memories—the sweet memories before the tragedy? How do you think that scene would have emotionally impacted the characters and viewers if Agatha said those words to Lara and John in a crowded Starbuck's? Don't answer that.

Here's an assignment for you: Watch one of your favorite movies or read one of your favorite novels. Jot down the setting of every scene *and* the emotional connection (if any) to each and every place for the POV character of that scene. You may find there isn't much—or you may start noticing how a great writer will create "connected settings" for strongest impact.

Choose the Best Place for Your High Moment

Whether setting is a huge element in your story because of your premise or not, you can make setting powerful and impacting by choosing each place carefully. For each scene, consider your high moment and the plot point you are going to reveal. Consider the dynamics and conflict of the characters in that scene and ask: Where can I put these characters to generate the most conflict (inner and outer) and the strongest emotional quotient?

You want every scene to have the highest EQ (Emotional Quotient) possible. Why? Because conflict is story, and emotions are needed for conflict. And strong emotions are needed for strong conflict and high stakes. If your characters feel nothing at all for the place they are in—guess what? The readers won't care either. You may not think that matters, but it does. Do you care where you live? Where you work? Where you spend your free time? Does place matter at all to you at anytime? Never? Are you human? Hmmm . . . I wonder.

One Last Very Important Thing

There's one more important aspect to setting, and one that hardly any writing instructors mention—unless they are telling writers to avoid dealing with it. But this is a component in novels that I personally feel is crucial and largely ignored: weather.

Weather is important! I mentioned how many writers ignore setting, often completely neglecting to show where their characters are in many of their scenes. That's like erasing the world and having people floating in space (which is also a setting, so I suppose they would be floating in nothing). They need to be shown where they are and why and how they feel about each and every place in your novel.

And that is how I feel about the weather. Weather is boring, you say? Really? Are you completely unaffected by a thunderstorm on a hot summer night? A tornado or hurricane headed your way? The crisp fall air in the Northeast, with the trees exploding in color? What about being at the top of a ski slope in a whiteout, snow blinding you and freezing your face and hands?

Weather Is Not (or Should Not) Be Boring

Just as you need to spend time thinking up creative settings, you need to spend as much time crafting the weather in your novel. Characters, like real people, react to weather in those same ways they react to place. We have memories and emotional connections with different types of weather. Weather triggers very strong memories, just as a place or a smell or a sound might. Weather can make our hearts soar with joy or catapult us into deep depression.

Use weather wisely. Let it affect your characters' moods and behavior. Let it impact the plot, create complications. Weather can cause delays and accidents. It can obscure vision, or make someone weak or faint. Weather is a terrific tool and—need I mention again?—needs to be shown and filtered through the POV character's mind-set.

Some settings come with a specific "weather package," and if so, you need to show it fully. If your story is set near the North Pole or in a thick rainforest, that weather is going to play a huge part in your scenes.

Load Up on Sensory Details

Don't ignore setting, and don't ignore weather. Let the reader know, richly and fully, exactly where and when your character is. Show how the place and the weather feel, smell, sound, and even taste. Establish and ground each scene quickly in place and weather, then use both those elements to generate emotion and conflict in the interests of your plot. Don't be boring and just throw out a line here and there about the weather just because you feel you have to!

This wraps up our look at the seventh pillar of novel construction. You now get your inspection checklist! Use all these checklists to help you inspect the construction of your novel, to make sure it will stand up under that weight of scrutiny and be a strong, long-lasting, and powerful story. Photocopy the checklist or type this link into your Internet browser: http://bit.ly/1wmYwRO.

Inspection Checklist #7
Setting with a Purpose

Question #1:

Have you deliberately chosen a setting/locale for your novel? Why this place and not another? Consider whether another might be more fresh/unique.

Question #2:

For every scene, have you asked: "Is this the best setting I can put my characters in?" Can you think of more original settings for some of your scenes? If so, use them.

Question #3:

What is your main character's connection with the settings in your novel? Can you make the emotions deeper and more meaningful?

Question #4:

What important past events can you come up with that tie your characters to your settings? Can you bring that into your story?

Question #5:

How many "boring" settings do you have in which characters stand or sit around and talk? How many can you change to make the setting more interesting?

Question #6:

In what ways can you change the way your protagonist feels about the setting by what happens to her in your story?

Question #7:

What unusual things can you have your protagonist notice about the various settings she is in, colored by her mood and what is happening in the story?

Question #8:

Go through your scenes and check: Have you clearly established the weather, time of day, time of year? Does the weather fit the mood or purpose of the scene?

Question #9:

Do you establish your setting right away in every scene and through the POV character's eyes? Check that. Do you give strong sensory details?

Question #10:

Pick one place that has special significance for your protagonist. What happened there? How does she feel there? Can you put her there in important moments in your story?

Question #11:

Can you create a place/locale in your story that triggers your protagonist to feel sad? Afraid? Nostalgic? Reflective? Angry? Regretful? Guilty?

Question #12:

Can you come up with a significant moment in the climax and/or ending of your book that shows strong connection between your protagonist and the setting?

Pillar #8: Tension Ramped to the Max

Chapter 22: Infusing Your Novel with Tension

I hope I don't need to tell you why you need tension in your novel. If I do, then I suggest you stop reading this chapter and spend some time reading some writing craft books and blog posts on novel structure. I don't mean to be snarky here; this is sage advice. Too many manuscripts come across my desk completely void of tension. However, I assume that the reason is the writer just has no idea how to create tension on every page—which is what a writer should aim for.

Every page? Is that possible? Yes, it is. And as an author, I work hard toward that goal—to keep up a continual sense of tension, which creates anticipation and interest on the reader's part.

The Different Types of Tension

But how can an author create tension? Just what is tension, anyway? In real life, we avoid tension, often at all costs. We don't want to be tense, and we don't like tense situations—they stress us out. And we don't want others around us to be tense (although, some people are really into drama, and I can attest there are those who really love such drama and feed off it).

So let's break this down a bit. First, we need to look at two aspects of tension. There is the tension the characters feel as individuals, and then there is the overall tension in the story. Don't confuse action with tension. Don't confuse high drama and high stakes with tension. You can have the most exciting plot elements in the world—with car chase scenes and buildings blowing up and the threat of the end of the world and still completely lack any tension—as far as the reader is concerned.

So while you may be writing *about tense things that should make people feel tense* or you are showing characters under stress, that doesn't necessarily equate to your book's tension. Which is to say that the tension a writer should be aiming for is something *other* than making readers feeling uptight or worried.

Make Your Reader Tense

What we as writers want is tension *in the reader*. And that kind of tension is not dependent on what kind of action is going on in a story. Even the most subdued, quiet, nothing-seems-to-be-happening scene can have tension ramped to the max.

No, this doesn't mean we want our readers to be stressed-out—although if you are writing intense suspense, that probably is exactly your aim. The kind of tension we want readers to feel is a sense of heightened anticipation, interest, curiosity, excitement. This is a good kind of tension. Think of the tension in a tightrope. We want a reader's attention to be *taut*.

In other words, we want readers to care so much about what is going on that they are uncomfortable. And when someone is uncomfortable, they want to resolve whatever it is to the point at which they can again feel comfortable.

A Good Kind of Tense

It's not always a bad kind of discomfort we want to put in our novels, such as waiting at the doctor's office to get test results. I mean the kind of discomfort you feel when you are waiting for your best friend to walk out of the security area of the airport into your arms. The kind of tension you feel when you are listening for your child's name to be called out at the graduation ceremony. The kind of tension you feel as you wait to greet your new grandchild. It's a good-feeling tension. And readers love it.

It's the "high" I long for as a reader, and cherish in a great novel. And something I don't often experience. To me, what sets apart a so-so or good book from a terrific one is the tension created (in me) as I read the story. The more gripped (tense) I am, the more immersed I am in the world of the story, the happier I am.

The Secret to Tension

So what is the secret to creating that kind of tension in a novel? I'll tell you what is at the heart of great tension in a story, and I bet you won't be surprised at my answer: great characters. Characters with a lot of inner conflict that is continually present.

Sure, outer conflict will add to that tension. But if your readers don't care about what happens to your character—because you did not present and carefully showcase an empathetic, intriguing, vulnerable, engaging character—they won't have much interest in the story and won't feel that niggling need to know what happens next.

Let me just say this: without constant tension in your story, you won't have a story. We went over the pillar of novel construction all about conflict and high stakes. If there are no stakes, no risks, nothing for your protagonist to lose, then how can you have any tension? You can't. And you can't have a compelling story either. So tension *is* story. Outer conflict throughout *is* crucial.

And the inner conflict your characters struggle with also creates tension. If your characters aren't having problems making choices and don't have conflicting feelings, your scenes will lack tension.

Way too many scenes I critique show the characters going along in their everyday lives without anything bothering them. They are fairly happy, and they aren't dealing with any stressful situations. They meet their friends for coffee or stand around chatting about unimportant, trivial things. Trust me: these scenes have no tension and hence generate no interest whatsoever.

Keep in mind these important points about creating tension:

- First, create great characters who struggle with inner and outer conflict.

- Second, have a terrific plot that features lots of outer conflict (which creates outward tension in the story).

- Third, have those high stakes—high for the protagonist and ones that impact her goal for the book. High stakes are about *what the character cares passionately about*. This is the key. To create tension, then, you need your very empathetic characters, and particularly your protagonist, to be facing trouble with high stakes.

We covered all these things in our four corner pillars of novel construction, so if you need to go back over them, do so. Go over the checklists you've been given. If your corner pillars are strong, you are well on your way to creating great tension.

How to Ramp Up That Tension

Granted, you need these great characters in a well-designed and well-executed plot. But that is not all you need to have tension ramped to the max.

There are technical things you can do to help tighten the pacing. And then, to ramp tension to the max, you want to focus on microtension. What is microtension? Just as the prefix suggests, it's tension on a micro level, or in small, barely noticeable increments. Your big plot twists and reversals and surprises are macro-tension items. But microtension is achieved on a line-by-line basis.

Aim at Mastering Microtension

Microtension—a term and concept that literary agent Donald Maass pretty much coined and defined—is tension infused in every paragraph of your novel. Yes, it can be done. You can have tension oozing out of every page. Sure, you want moments when your readers feel anxious or worried for your characters because they care what happens to them. But true page-by-page tension is a combination of a terrifically executed compelling plot *and* writing that shows continual inner and outer conflict going on with all the characters.

For example, anytime a character has conflicting feelings, you have microtension. Microtension can be small, simmering, subtext, subtle. Even the choice of words or the turn of a phrase can produce microtension by its freshness or unexpected usage.

A sudden change in emotion can create tension. A character struggling between two opposite emotions creates tension. Odd contradictory emotions and reactions can create microtension.

Examples of Seeming Contradictions

Donald Maass, in his Breakout Novel workshop, had us participants thinking about how people often cry at weddings and feel a strange sadness. There can be a sense of loss at a wedding (a mother sad over "losing" her daughter, or missing the baby she raised, for example). It seems contradictory to cry and be sad at such a joyous occasion. (Now, if the mother hates the guy her daughter is marrying, she may cry justifiably, but that isn't microtension. If she struggles with trying to let go and trust her daughter will make it work amid her dislike of the guy, that is.)

At such joyous occasions, we also think about the loved ones we have lost, who aren't there to witness the event. Think about how many people get depressed during holiday season—which is supposed to be the "happy" time of year. Bright happiness shimmering around us often amplifies our grief and loneliness.

Then, Maass had us think how people often laugh at funerals or wakes. In honoring the recently departed, they will recount humorous anecdotes to make the mourners laugh and remember funny moments in the deceased's life. Isn't it odd? To laugh in joy over someone who is dead and whom we loved. It seems a contradiction, and it's curious, so it intrigues us.

At any given moment, we are feeling a number of different emotions, and they often clash. By going deep into your characters and drawing out that type of inner conflict as often as possible, you can bring microtension into your scenes. Again, you will have outer conflict as well (hopefully a lot of it). But by adding the inner conflict in such a way, you can ramp up the microtension. Try to avoid common expressions we've all heard before. Think past the obvious first emotion and find something deeper, something submerged and underlying the superficial emotion. Strive for the unexpected.

Three Areas in Which You Can Add Microtension

Here are three areas and ways in which you can add microtension to your scenes:

1. *Dialog*: examine each line of dialog. Take out boring and unnecessary words, and trivial matters. Go for clever. Find a way to give each speaker a unique voice and style of speaking (as we went over in the chapters on secondary characters, and which will be covered in upcoming chapters on voice). Keep in mind the tension is in the relationship between the characters speaking, *not* in the information presented.

2. *Action (physical)*: This can be with any kind of action—high or low. Even a gesture is action. So think about how to make an action incongruous. What does that mean? I've said repeatedly that real people are conflicted all the time. Real people are complex, inconsistent. So by having a character react in an incongruent manner, and having incongruent developments in the story line, that will add microtension. Have things happen and characters react in ways *the reader does not expect*. And most importantly, show everything through the POV character's emotions. Action will *not* be tense unless the character is experiencing it and emotionally reacting to it.

3. *Exposition*: Exposition is the prose, your writing. It's the way you explain what is happening as you show it. It includes internal monologue. Find ways to add those conflicted emotions and create dissonance. Show ideas at war with one another. Use word choices that can feel contradictory or imply subtext. Find fresh, different ways to describe common things.

Here's a random passage I grabbed out of Kathryn Magendie's amazing novel *Tender Graces*:

> When Grandmother Laudine drove up in her shiny black Chevrolet pickup truck with her umpteenth husband she'd asked us to call Uncle Runt, the rain had turned into the skinny stinging kind. I watched out the open door as Grandmother blobbered towards me. She hollered back to Runt and the storm took her words out of her mouth and scattered them to faraway places. Runt went back to the truck while Grandmother barreled into our living room. We kids lined up to get a good look at her.
>
> She wore a pink pantsuit with pockets the size of my head, tissues sticking up in one and a bottle of Milk of Magnesia in the other. Her britches stopped above her ankles, and she had on pink bobby socks with lace, and white tenny shoes with pink shoelaces. Her hair wasn't hers at all, but a big poofy wig that held raindrops like sparkly diamonds. When she hugged on me, she smelled like Vicks VapoRub.

Magendie could have written all that in a very expected, common, boring way. But look at how she twists words in new ways, all the while giving such insight into her POV character with a unique voice and way of looking at her world. Not all of us are such gifted wordsmiths as she, but we can all take time to rework our exposition, dialog, and actions to be so much more interesting, and that will generate microtension. I find her books almost impossible to put down because of the originality and genuineness of her exposition (among many other things).

How Much Is Too Much?

Can you have too much tension or microtension? Too much conflict? If it's done well and it's meaningful, I would say no. Examine every page of your novel. In fact, one suggestion Maass gave us was to throw our pages in the air and randomly pick them up, then work on adding microtension to each page, out of order. This is a line-by-line tension, and if you can infuse each page with it, adding to the overall tension of your story and the tension your characters are feeling due to inner conflict, you will have a page-turner.

You now have a good idea of why you need tension in your novel and how to ramp it up, so here is your next checklist. Be sure to go over all the groups of questions to make sure you've ramped your tension to the max. Photocopy the checklist or type this link into your Internet browser: http://bit.ly/16wgS9i.

Inspection Checklist #8
Tension Ramped to the Max

Question #1:

What is the central *inner* conflict your protagonist is dealing with as it pertains to your concept? Can you increase it?

Question #2:

Look through each scene. What is the key conflict in it? How can you make it more complex? Make the characters more conflicted?

Question #3:

Can you find a moment for each of your main characters to want the opposite of their heart's desire? Can you make it bigger, more emotional?

Question #4:

Go through all your dialog. Can you find places to add subtext and mystery? Tighten and make it fresher?

Question #5:

Print out your novel and toss the pages. Pick up ten pages. Can you find five places on each page in which to add microtension? Repeat.

Question #6:

Where can you have characters say something other than what they mean (subtext)? Hint at something secret?

Question #7:

Can you find/add five places in your novel where a character acts rashly, inconsistently, contrary? Ten places?

Question #8:

Can you find/add at least one place in each scene where the character thinks, reacts, or does something wholly unexpected?

Question #9:

Look for high-action passages where tension should be high. Are the sentences short, packed with strong words, and showing strong emotion?

Question #10:

Find your lowest-tension scenes. How can you make your protagonist more conflicted emotionally to ramp up the tension?

Question #11:

Do you have any scenes in which everyone is happy and all is well? What monkey wrench you can throw in to upend things?

Question #12:

Have you gone through your latest draft to eliminate extraneous, boring, flat words and phrasing? If not, do so!

Pillar #9: Dialog—Compressed and Essential

Chapter 23: Constructing Strong, Believable Dialog

Dialog is the element that brings stories to life. Imagine reading an entire novel void of dialog. Trying to sustain a whole novel—or even a few consecutive scenes—without any dialog would be difficult, for that would mean your story would have to be conveyed by narrative and internal thoughts alone. So our ninth essential pillar of novel construction is all about dialog.

Writing great dialog is challenging. Browne and King, in their terrific book *Self-Editing for Fiction Writers*, tell how some editors considering a manuscript for publication look first at the dialog. One unnamed editor is quoted as saying, "If the dialog doesn't work, the manuscript gets bounced. If it's good, I start reading."

People are social and they communicate—often not very well. But speak, they do. Unless your character is isolated, which is justified in many stories (as the result of shipwreck or solo exploration, etc.), he is going to talk to other people. And frequently, in such stories, the sole character ends up talking out loud to himself a lot, in dialog, as if to another person. Or to God, or even to a volleyball (as in the movie *Castaway*).

First, Avoid Boring

So, although we want the dialog in our scenes—like every other component—to be believable and feel "natural," the tendency for many writers is to write boring dialog.

Just as everyday people and situations can be boring, so too can dialog. But, as I've said many times before, readers don't want "boring." They read to be entertained, inspired, excited, moved, and changed.

Yet, we need a balance between boring and ridiculous. Dialog that is over-stylized, overly stiff, or unnatural is jarring if it's "out of character." The key to "proper" dialog lies with the characters who are speaking.

Know Thy Characters

We'll be looking at the concept of voice in the next chapter, but it's important here to understand some things about voice. Many think that voice has to do with the author's writing style. It doesn't. Voice is character. Each POV character in your novel has his or her own voice—an individual style of speaking and thinking.

I bring this up here to help you keep in mind that, yes, the speech of each character needs to be true and appropriate, tailored to personality, background, education, ethnicity, geographical location, etc. But so does the inner voice. When you are in POV, in a character's head, she is not going to think and react to events with one kind of voice and vocalize in another kind.

So while I'm not going to go into voice in this discussion of dialog, keep this important fact in the back of your mind. It's not hard to have a character think a direct thought in his style of speaking, but it's a little harder to do so with the running narrative in his POV.

Some Basics on Crafting Great Dialog

- The first point of emphasis regarding the creation of great dialog is *making sure it fits the context and the character.*

- Next: *No one should sound like anyone else.* Unless you have some funny bit about a character mimicking another character, each person should be unique. It takes work to stylize character, and we've already gone over some of this in the previous posts on creating great secondary characters. So apply all those things you've learned to the character's dialog—the way she phrases words and constructs sentences, the word whiskers she may use, and the kinds of things she talks about.

171

- *Don't use dialog to dump information.* All too often writers use dialog as a way to impart information to the reader. Yes, dialog is a great way to convey important things related to your plot and backstory. Through dialog you can nicely reveal the past and character motivation. But when you slip into what is sometimes called "As you know, Bob" dialog, the reader can tell you are having characters say things they obviously would know already. Those lines smack of "info dump," put in there for the reader's benefit. Which is a no-no.

- *Don't tell us things we already know or don't care about.* Many beginning writers make the mistake of needless repetition. They might say something in the narrative, and then have a character speak out loud the very same thing. For example: Mary really hated it when people talked down to her. She looked at George and said, "You know, George, I really hate it when people talk down to me."

Okay, that's a bit obvious, but you get the point, right? And often writers have excessive amounts of mundane, boring dialog due to trying to make the conversation sound natural (as I noted earlier). Trivial conversing over the weather or what someone had for breakfast is not going to interest readers. But then, how do you show your characters talking in a believable way, when we *do* talk about things like that?

The trick to great dialog, as hinted at by the title of this pillar of novel construction, is to *compress* the dialog. Just what does that mean? Here are some ways:

- *Avoid "on the nose" dialog.* This means that characters should never simply state exactly what's on their minds, without nuance or subtext, nor appear to be giving "exposition." In real life, people rarely say directly what's on their minds. Our fictional characters should reflect that.

- *Less is more.* If you can "say" the same thing with a visual image, action, behavior, or sound effect instead of through dialog, omit the dialog. Trim out extra words, boring bits of info and phrasing. Tighten a sentence like "I was wondering how you

172

might be feeling today, seeing as you had recently undergone surgery and might be a bit under the weather" to "Hey, how's it going? You better? Sore?" Think about the content, what you need your character to convey, then tailor it and tighten it to best represent his personality and unique voice.

- *Have a specific purpose for what's being said,* and lead steadily to your point. Don't have random chatting that serves no purpose. I like to think of every page of my (usually very long) novels as precious, expensive real estate. Every word should count. Every line of dialog should have a point to it.

There is so much more to crafting great dialog, but this general overview should give you some things to consider. Start going through your scenes and look at the dialog. Read it out loud. You'll hear the clunky, boring bits (I hope). Take those out. If you need to have characters introduced or say hello, just note that with a short line of narrative or dialog, then move on quickly to what it important in your scene.

Creating Engaging Dialog by Using Subtext

Just what is subtext? Subtext refers to the thoughts that the character is *not* saying—ideas that are being suggested but not actually voiced directly. They are below (sub) the text.

Real people use subtext constantly. We almost never really say what we mean or voice what we really want. We hide our feelings and cover with expressions and words that imply something other. We do this to protect ourselves or to present a certain impression. Or we might not even know what we are truly feeling. And we sometimes lie to ourselves. All this is fodder for subtext.

I would venture to say that real people use subtext more often than not in everything they say. Pay attention to people's conversations (without being obvious or invading privacy). You can learn a lot about subtext by doing this (and hearing yourself!).

Wow, that means writers who want to create realistic dialog are going to have to work on crafting subtext in their dialog. It's not always easy to do, but I'm going to give you some suggestions on how to do this well.

First write your scene and have characters say outright what they want and mean. Then go through and change the wording so that they aren't saying those things. One way you can do this is by having a character talk about something *other*, while your narrative is revealing she is trying to say something else. Example (Before and After):

> "John, I'm worried that you don't really love me."
>
> "Mary, you're right. I really don't. But I have to keep up appearances. We don't want the children to think anything's wrong."
>
> "Well, that really hurts. I guess I'll have to just accept that fact and pretend I don't care."

Okay, I hope you see how unreal this is, even though this is the truth of how John and Mary feel.

Here's the same exchange but with these feelings as subtext:

> "John, are you listening?" Mary fidgeted, her heart aching at the way he was ignoring her.
>
> "What? Oh, sure. Why are you wondering if I love you? Of course I do—how could you think such a thing?" John went back to reading his book, his brows furrowed in concentration. Mary waited for more, but he said nothing else. Then his face brightened. "Hey, what's for dessert?"
>
> "Chocolate cake—your favorite." She played with her apron strings, then, with clenched teeth, she threw the apron to the ground. "I'll go get you a piece."

Mary isn't saying what she really feels, but we can tell by her show of emotion.

You can go through and find lines of dialog that are too direct in telling what a character feels or wants and then have her say something unrelated to what's important, as a way to cover her feelings.

Here are two other ways to craft compressed, essential dialog:

1. Put in moments of silence. Silence implies other feelings and thoughts. When a character pauses, doesn't answer right away and gives some emotional "tell" with a gesture or expression, that is subtext.

174

2. Tension can thicken when characters *do* talk about mundane things but the reader knows there is something very intense going on plot-wise or unspoken between them. Again, the characters' physical movements, tone of voice, and behavior can belie what they are actually saying.

When you have characters constantly in conflict with each other and experiencing inner conflict, the result is a lot of subtext that comes across in dialog. A character who is struggling with feelings may blurt out the truth, but often it's only a partial truth. There is so much more being left unsaid.

So think about the things your character isn't saying and why. You might have her think some of this as internal direct thoughts, if she really knows how she feels. But even in the internal dialog with herself, she may not be thinking what she really feels. The more you can have her physical actions and reactions show something inconsistent with what she vocalizes, the more that conflict will come through.

Subtext, then, really is all about conflict.

Some Technical Suggestions

Regarding writing dialog of any kind, here are some tips to making it flow smoothly:

- *Don't go on for more than five or six lines of dialog between characters without making it clear who is speaking.* With only two people speaking, after a while it's hard to keep track of who is talking. Just adding "Mary said" here and there can help avoid confusion. With more than two conversing, it's essential you make it clear with every line who the speaker is.

- *Conversely, don't use a speaker tag with every line.* Remove unnecessary speaker tags. If it's clear who is speaking, you don't need one. A narrative tag here or there will suffice. Example: John shook his head. "I really don't care."

- *Put a character's speech and action together in a paragraph.* Failure to do this causes confusion as to who is speaking. It's assumed the last person mentioned is the speaker, so if you do not group the

175

speech and action for each character in separate paragraphs, you'll have the wrong characters speaking your lines.

- *Don't use fancy verbs for speech* (speaker tags). Just use *said, asked, replied,* or *answered.* Once in a while you might punch with a different verb: "There," she declared. "I found it." Speaker tags should be functional and invisible. Readers *blip* over the word *said.* And that's what you want.

- *Don't use adverbs with your speaker tags.* You've probably heard this, but it's a good admonition. A good writer will *show* the intent and emotion in what's being said and with body language. Instead of writing "'Go away,' he said angrily," write "'Go away,' he said, clenching his fists, his face flushing with heat."

- *Read it aloud.* You will hear the wordiness or stiffness of dialog by doing this. It helps a lot.

- *Use contractions where appropriate.* Unless it befits the character to speak without using contractions (*it's* instead of *it is,* for example), be sure to use them.

Really, writing great dialog that is compressed and essential is all about showing, not telling. Instead of telling via speaker or narrative tags what someone is feeling, show with gestures, tone, expression, and body language. Not sure how and in what quantity to do this? Pull out some of your favorite novels and highlight the lines that show that emotion, which will also come across as subtext under the "other" things being said.

By studying authors who do this well, you will get a feel for how to do this. One book that really impressed me with deftly wielded subtext was Joan Didion's *A Book of Common Prayer.* Her characters, all with conflicting needs, hardly ever say what they really feel or want. The dialog is snappy and fresh, with characters interrupting one another and talking about completely other things than what they are really thinking or care about.

Ready for your next checklist? Photocopy the checklist or type this link into your Internet browser: http://bit.ly/1x41lJr.

Next up—Pillar #10: Voice—Unique for Each Character.

Inspection Checklist #9
Dialog—Compressed and Essential

Question #1:

Go through all your dialog. Have you tightened and trimmed to condense, removing all boring, mundane, and unimportant lines?

Question #2:

Have you gone through and removed all unnecessary speaker tags? Conversely, have you made sure it's clear who is speaking?

Question #3:

Have you made sure to alternate speaker tags with narrative bits to show both who is speaking and what the tone, mood, reaction, or emotion is?

Question #4:

Have you made sure each line of dialog well reflects each character's personality, background, education, and ethnicity?

Question #5:

Have you checked to ensure none of your dialog is used as an info dump, telling readers what either they or the characters already know?

Question #6:

Have you removed or changed all "on the nose" dialog—characters saying exactly what they are feeling? Replaced with subtext and implication?

Question #7:

Have you removed all adverbs in speaker tags and instead found a way to *show* the emotion of the character as she speaks?

Question #8:

Does every spoken line in your scenes serve a purpose? Help to reveal character or a new plot development? If not, change or take it out.

Question #9:

Have you found places where you can insert moments of silence to add tension? Find some more.

Question #10:

Have you checked to make sure each character's speech and actions are grouped together in paragraphs to make clear who is speaking?

Question #11:

Have you gone through and removed excessive "flowery" speaker tag verbs such as cajoled, postulated, and elucidated?

Question #12:

Have you checked to make sure your characters speak naturally, using contractions where needed?

Pillar #10: Voice—Unique for Each Character

Chapter 24: Creating Strong Voices in Your Novel

We're about to look at the last three pillars of novel construction in this book. These last three—voice, writing style, and motifs—are important elements in a novel, but there are no specific "rules" governing them. No one can tell you what your writing style should be, for example, but there are some guidelines I can share with you that will help you make decisions about your writing style, or the kind of voice you give your characters, or the kinds of motifs you may or may not want to inject into your story.

There are many other small components that make a novel great, such as attention to detail; creative use of metaphor or symbolism; and technical issues, such as sentence, paragraph, and scene length. All these things are mostly a matter of personal taste, although often formed and restricted in some way by genre.

The key things to keep in mind with all these elements are these:

- Everything you "build" your novel with—every board, nail, and pipe—needs to serve a purpose, a specific function. There shouldn't be random, useless materials thrown into the construction of a house. Similarly, as you build your novel, it makes no sense to throw in anything—scenes, settings, bits of dialog, plot developments, extraneous characters—that don't serve the needs of your premise.

- Genre plays a big part in dictating the type of pillars you construct your novel with. Maybe that seems unnecessary to say, for you wouldn't come up with a sci-fi concept and then write a story that has no elements of sci-fi in it. But genre is more than just a way to pigeonhole a book's subject matter. Readers of genres have certain expectations, and all the components of a novel have to fit within reader expectations to some degree. If you are writing a dark noir comedy, your voice and writing style and dialog and scene construction should match that of novels in the genre.

- Some of your secondary pillars are going to be bigger and stronger and structurally support your story more than others based on the kind of story you tell. I use a lot of motifs in my novels, for example, whether they are fantasy or psychological suspense or relational dramas. You may find little use for motifs and symbolism in your novels. I believe using motifs provides more structural support for any novel, but your "house" won't collapse if you don't use any.

With that said, We'll take a brief look at these last three pillars to wrap up the essential pillars of novel construction, which will end with your having twelve in-depth inspection checklists to help you construct the best novels you possibly can.

Just What Is Voice?

I mentioned in the last chapter that voice belongs to your characters, not you. That may sound contradictory to what you've been taught or what you've seen written in blogs or writing craft books. I've heard various definitions of what "voice" is in a novel, and it is often referring to writing style. I do not embrace that definition, and I'll explain why.

First, writing style is writing style. It is not tone or voice. It's the way you put words together to create sentences. It is the choice of words you use and how you convey your ideas and characters and dialog. And because both writing style and voice are important, they each are a separate pillar of novel construction.

Voice is something entirely different from writing style, as far as it concerns this pillar of construction.

Don't Confuse Voice with Writing Style

One article I found online says voice applies only with a first-person narrator—her persona. And here we have Donald Maass, in his book *Writing the Breakout Novel*, sharing these thoughts:

> "I am looking for authors with a distinctive voice." I hear that from editors over lunch almost as often as I hear, "I am looking for big, well-written thrillers."
>
> What the heck is "voice"? By this, do editors mean "style"? I do not think so. By voice, I think they mean not only a unique way of putting words together but a unique sensibility, a distinctive way of looking at the world, an outlook that enriches an author's oeuvre. They want to read an author who is like no other. An original. A standout. A voice.

This, again, to me is dealing with writing style. Maass disagrees with that assessment, and hence creates a lot of confusion (in my humble opinion). And agents and editors that throw the term "voice" around, confusing it with writing style, make matters worse.

Take a look at what Maass goes on to say, and tell me if it confuses you or makes the issue clearer:

> How can you develop your voice? To some extent it happens all by itself. Stories come from the subconscious. What drives you to write, to some extent, are your own unresolved inner conflicts. Have you noticed your favorite authors have character types that recur? Plot turns that feel familiar? Descriptive details that you would swear you have read before (a yellow bowl, a slant of light, an inch of cigarette ash)? That is the subconscious at work.
>
> You can facilitate voice by giving yourself the freedom to say things in your own unique way. You do not talk exactly like anyone else, right? Why should you write like everyone else?

Again, to me, this is all about writing style. We bring into our writing who we are, how we think, what moves and influences and scares us. And I am not of the school to let "voice" or writing style just "happen all by itself." Just as with constructing any of the other eleven pillars essential for building a strong novel, voice shouldn't be left up to chance, fate, serendipity, whim, or some subconscious leaning (my apologies to Donald Maass—I hardly ever disagree with him!).

Let me say this in simple terms—and this is my take on the whole "voice vs. writing style" issue: voice is all about characters—not about you.

I think my way of looking at these two novel components makes more sense, and makes it easier for writers to both grasp the concepts and work with them constructively (since we're all about construction!).

Every character in your novel has his or her own voice, whether a child, a man or woman, a dog, or a robot. In addition, every POV character in your novel has both a unique speaking voice and internal voice (which is shown in the way each thinks).

Voice Isn't Just Speech

Any character that speaks out loud (not a POV character) has a voice. I don't mean literally here—for of course all characters have a voice if they can speak (and if they use sign language, that's speech too). Conversely, a POV character might be mute, but she would still have a voice because the reader can hear what she is thinking in her head.

What we're talking about pertains to the manner, style, and presentation of that speech. With non-POV characters, their voice comes out only in the words they actually say and how they're said—since the writer is not going into their heads. We looked at that when examining the last pillar on dialog.

With POV characters, voice embodies more than spoken words or direct thoughts in their heads. The narrative should reflect that voice as well. When you craft a scene in a character's POV, every line in that scene has to feel as though it is being processed, chewed, and spit out by that character. Everything that happens in that scene is witnessed, experienced, felt, and reacted to by that character. And so, even the narrative must have "voice."

Narrative Must Be Shaped by Voice

Think about writing a scene in the POV of a six-year-old girl who is a spoiled, rich only child. Let's say the scene takes place at the dinner table, and while she is eating, her parents get in an argument about money, and the father says she will not be allowed to take ballet anymore, and then smacks her precious puppy when it tries to get a piece of meat from off the table.

That narrative must sound like a six-year-old rich spoiled girl's voice. She is going to notice, react, and think her age. She isn't going to comment on the subtle nuances of her parents' argument. She's going to be confused and upset as to why she can't take ballet, and she's going to be mad and scared when her father hits her dog. She will not use an adult vocabulary or think obtusely, abstractly, or with metaphor. The reader should feel and wholly believe she is experiencing and reacting to all that happens in the scene (and there should be a good reason to use her as a POV character too).

All too often I find in the novels I edit and critique scenes in a character's POV that does not have the appropriate voice. Children sound like adults. Old women sound like young men. Often all the characters sound just like the author—or so it seems to me.

So much goes into voice: education, background, past pain, fears, likes and dislikes, opinions, personality traits, ethnicity, and so on. Just like dialog. In fact, if you can think of voice as just an extension of dialog—as the POV character speaking through the entire narrative of the scene—it may help you to get a handle on voice.

Getting into Character

One thing that helps me with voice is to pretend I'm the character. I try to immerse myself so much into the role as I'm writing the scene that I *am* that character. This is what actors do—they get into character. Some actors say that when they're shooting a movie, they stay in character all the time—even when they leave the set and go home for the night.

Which makes me think of a funny bit on one of the DVDs for *The Lord of the Rings*, which showed director Peter Jackson's amazement when he heard actor Brad Dourif (Wormtongue) speak in an American Southern drawl, thinking the actor was just joking around (he wasn't; that was his "real" voice). In the films, Dourif's character has a kind of rich British accent. Clearly, Dourif stayed "in character" while not filming, which no doubt helped him do such a terrific job in creating the voice of Wormtongue. And, here too, I'm not just talking about his accent. That voice went deep into character, shown through his inflection, mannerisms, facial expressions, and tone. All this relates to voice.

Voice Isn't Just How Someone Sounds

So as you richly develop all the characters in your novel—and we've looked at many ways on how to do this with both your protagonist and your secondary characters—be sure to spend a good amount of time on voice. Not just thinking about how the character sounds when she talks out loud but how *who she is* shapes and determines her mind-set—what and how she thinks about things.

In order to construct a strong novel, those character pillars must be made of unique, believable characters. By spending time giving those characters a rich past and a core need, a deep-seated fear, and a lie they believe, you will have characters that jump off the page. But . . . if you do not give them the appropriate voice, those pillars will crumble.

As I mentioned in the example above of the six-year-old girl—if you, the author, *intrude* in the scene by narrating or showing a character thinking in a style that does not fit who she is, the reader will notice. Yes, it's a challenge to write every word in every scene in POV, but that's required with either a first-person or third-person POV. And this is one of the biggest flaws I see in novels.

If you are going to use an omniscient voice to tell the story, you can slip in and out of voices as you portray the different characters, and in addition, you have the narrator's omniscient storytelling voice over all (which must be developed in the same way as any other character's voice). Not many writers can pull off an omniscient voice well, and the downside and challenge to using such a voice is its tendency to distance the reader and *tell* the story rather than show it. And as most of us have been taught, readers these days don't want to be told stories; they want to see them happening before their eyes, through the eyes of the POV characters.

So think of voice as each character's voice: unique and specific. The writing style of a scene will be influenced and shaped by that voice, but there is more to writing style than just that—which we'll start exploring in the next chapter that covers our eleventh pillar.

It's checklist time! Photocopy the checklist or type this link into your Internet browser: http://bit.ly/1zCM8gf.

Inspection Checklist #10
Voice—Unique for Each Character

Question #1:

Have you gone through and thoroughly developed all your characters and created a speaking style for them?

Question #2:

Have you gone through and thoroughly developed all your POV characters and created a narrative voice style?

Question #3:

Have you checked to make sure each character's speaking voice and POV narrative voice sound similar in all your scenes?

Question #4:

Are the voices for your POV characters correct for their age, and is this reflected in the narrative?

Question #5:

Think about each character's "word whiskers" or special phrases. Have you pulled those into the POV narrative?

Question #6:

Does the narrative of each scene reflect and reveal the mind-set or attitude of the POV character?

Question #7:

Does the narrative of each scene reflect and reveal the mood and emotion of the POV character?

Question #8:

Is your POV narrative voice void of vocabulary that your character would not use in his thoughts or speech?

Question #9:

For your POV characters: How is their speech shaped by where they grew up, their education, ethnicity, and status?

Question #10:

If you are writing in first person POV, what are some ways you have made this a unique and compelling voice?

Question #11:

Have you checked through all your scenes to make sure there is no author intrusion—narrating "out of POV"?

Question #12:

If you are writing in omniscient voice, have you developed a unique narrative voice that feels like a character in your book?

Pillar #11: Writing Style—Concise and Specific

Chapter 25: Finding Your Special Writing Style

In the last chapter, we looked at voice, which tied back into character development. I made the distinction between what some call the "author's voice" and what I feel truly is voice in a novel—specifically the voice of the POV characters. Just as each character has a specific and unique speaking voice, each should have an internal narrative voice that is consistent with his spoken voice.

So where does writing style fit in? I believe that "voice" is all about characters, whereas writing style is all about how writers present the story in all its components. The choices a writer makes as to scene structure and style; length of sentences, paragraphs, and chapters; and the sophistication (or not) of vocabulary and word choice and literary devices (such as metaphor, similes, anaphora) comes under the "heading" of writing style.

No doubt you have some favorite authors, and it's likely that one thing that you love about their books is their writing style. A lot of commercial authors, to me, have a very simplistic—almost superficial—writing style. Certain genres, surely, gravitate toward those types of styles. Personally, I find a lot of commercial novels very boring to read. They may have great premises and promise exciting plots. But it's hard for me to get engaged if the writing is flat and mechanical. I see this a lot in the mystery/suspense genre, for example. Sometimes I feel I could take ten best sellers by ten different authors and not be able to differentiate between them. They all sound alike to me.

188

I'm not saying that's a bad thing—writing styles are a matter of taste. I love creative, unusual, evocative writing. There are a lot of best-selling novels out there I can't stomach, but clearly someone can. A lot of someones!

So, when considering this pillar of novel construction, knowing you need to have *some* writing style, what do you need to consider?

This eleventh pillar of novel construction is called Writing Style—Concise and Specific, so let's delve into this topic and explore what it means to be both concise and specific.

What Does It Mean to Be Specific?

First, think about the genre you are writing in. Genre determines a lot. Novels are a commodity—a product you are producing for a consumer, a reader. When you describe your novel on sites that sell your book, you have to provide a description for it, as well as fiction categories and keywords. All this is a way to accurately define your novel so a reader can see what you are marketing to him, and with this information decide to purchase your product or not.

You may find this a distasteful way to think of your novel, but it's not far off from how a literary agent or publisher is going to consider your book. For the bottom line in this publishing industry is "will this novel sell and who will it sell to?"

If you are writing a novel for your own enjoyment or plan to publish it or print it out off your computer just for friends or family, that's a different matter. In that case, you may care little about whether your writing style fits a certain genre. You may not care about genre at all. And that, too, is fine. It's all about why you are writing novels and what you want to do with them.

This may seem a bit off track from our pillar on writing style, but I think it's important for a writer to first make some very specific determinations. Ask:

- Whom are you writing this novel for? Just for yourself or friends? Or do you plan to publish it?

- How important is it to you to sell well (whatever that means to you)?

- Are you interested in branding yourself and your writing style in order to become known for a certain type of style/genre/story?

Genre Plays a Big Part in Determining Writing Style

The answers to these questions are important because if you hope for commercial success, you are going to have to tailor your writing style *somewhat* to be similar to other authors writing in the same genre. If you write in different genres, as I do, each novel will have a different writing style, to a certain extent.

My fantasy publisher read my relational drama/mystery *Someone to Blame* and told me he would never have guessed I had written that novel. My writing style was so different from my adult fairy tales, and rightly so. With my mysteries, I write in a tighter, terser style, as would be expected with that genre. I love writing fantasy because I can "let loose" with my words and go deeper with metaphor and creative use of vocabulary. I might have wind snap and snarl and tangle water into knots in my fantasy series, but in my mysteries wind and water aren't depicted so imaginatively. That's not to say I dumb down my writing or try to be plain and boring. I still aim for a unique, expressive, and evocative writing style—with every novel I write. But my first consideration is genre and audience.

Write to Fit the Genre

As I said, readers have expectations. A consumer reads about a product and expects it to deliver as promised. When you put a book up for sale online and describe it as a cozy mystery, readers are going to expect your novel to have a writing style that fits within certain parameters. The best way to determine what the parameters are for a particular genre or subgenre is to study a lot of novels in those genres.

This may seem silly to suggest. Obvious, right? Well, a lot of beginning novelists write books in a style that does not fit the genre well at all. And this becomes a fatal flaw for their book's success.

Writing to fit genre is one consideration when constructing this pillar. Being specific entails knowing your intended audience and readers' expectations when it comes to writing style. Your job as the author is to meet their expectations.

I believe there probably is an audience for just about any writing style, and if you are writing literary fiction, sometimes there are few rules and even fewer expectations. I've read books (best sellers) that have one paragraph chapters or a paragraph that goes on for pages. Yes, you can write any old way you like, but you need to keep in mind whom you are writing for and what genre you are writing in.

This is just the first consideration.

Start by Imitation

Often, when learning to write a novel, a writer may spend countless hours focusing on getting all the basics in hand: plot, structure, characters, and all those tricky components that take time to master. Usually writing style is ignored at first, and a writer's early attempts to simply get words on the page are often clunky and/or derivative. And that's part of the growing process.

Just as a toddler begins to speak by listening to and imitating the adults who speak to him, a new writer will often try to copy the writing style of other authors. Which is a great thing to do—at first. It's said "imitation is the best form of flattery," but it's also a smart way to learn. By studying and imitating the writing style of great writers in your genre, you can get a feel of how to write your stories.

Emulation Is Fine for a Time

But at some point, you will have to let go of your tightly gripping hand and cross the street by yourself. There is probably no magic moment in which you suddenly have your own writing style, but I can recall many moments when I felt my unique way of writing beginning to emerge. I started taking chances, letting my imagination wander freely. I shut off the infernal internal editor and knocked the writing instructor off my shoulder and experimented.

More and more moments came to me in which I was writing freely with my own flair, unhindered and unburdened by all the "supposed tos" that were nagging me from the bleachers. I think by about my fifth novel I hit my stride. It was during the writing of *The Map across Time* that I felt I had found my writing style. I was in my groove. I had settled happily and comfortably into my writing style. And the cool thing was, it carried over into all my subsequent novels of various genres.

It's Just a Learning Curve

This process is not all that dissimilar to learning to dance or do gymnastics or play basketball. There is a huge learning curve at first, but with diligence and a measure of talent and ability, you "get the hang of it."

Note, though, this is not something you get and then are stuck with. It's not like the birth of a baby, which, after it's born, you don't get to send back and revise. Your writing style is fluid, versatile, adaptive. Or it should be. And even better is the fact that you can have multitudes of various styles—as many as you like.

I'm in a unique position as a writing coach. I see these various stages beginning writers are in, and how they are attempting to develop a writing style. I often see writing that is very derivative or clearly structured to impress or to sound intelligent or clever. All in all, much of this comes across fake, forced, or awkward.

To Thine Own Self . . .

What's the key to finding and developing your unique writing style? I think a lot of it has to do with being true to yourself. Ugh, I know how that sounds. Yes, you may at first emulate other authors' writing styles. But there comes a point when you need to break through that wall separating you from them to establish your own special style.

So how do you know if you are being "true to yourself"? This may sound a bit New Agey, but I believe, as does author Elizabeth George, that if you listen to your body, it will tell you whether what you are writing feels true or not.

What I'm saying, in essence, is when you write, try to listen to what your body is telling you. It will be honest with you.

Have you ever written a passage you really liked and wanted to use, but you had this nagging feeling it didn't work? Then, when you squelched that warning and shared your passage with your critique team, what happened? They all responded the same way. It doesn't work, they said. It feels wrong. Maybe they had more specific responses for you that helped you see why and in what ways that passage didn't work. But, hey, you already knew that. Or, you would have, had you listened to what your body was telling you.

There's an uneasy feeling of discomfort a seasoned writer gets when she veers away from a true and honest writing voice and starts forcing the style for one reason or another. Then again, a writer can just get burned out, or have days or weeks in which she feels uncreative and can't seem to come up with effective prose that feels like her true style.

Lots of Ways to Inspire a Beautiful Writing Style

There are lots of ways to inspire creativity, to prompt ideas and the flow of beautiful writing. My favorite way, which I also picked up from Elizabeth George, is to try to read something terrific before I start writing. A half an hour prep time spent reading a great author's exquisite prose can often inspire you and jumpstart your stalled creative flow.

This doesn't mean you won't have to go back and diligently work on your passages. Fine-tuning by substituting word choices or coming up with similes or a catchy turn of phrase is part of honing your writing style.

You've probably heard the adage "garbage in, garbage out." And then there's "you are what you eat"—which could be rewritten to "you write what you read." Keep in mind that reading a lot of drivel (you can determine what constitutes that) can adversely affect your writing.

You may have thought I'd be teaching you how to come up with a great writing style all your own. Sorry, that is something you will have to do. But by studying hard and emulating great writers, you will be on your way. Then, it's a journey of many miles—not just a few blocks. Give yourself permission to let yourself go in your writing—perhaps freewrite, experiment with different tenses or tones, or use writing prompts to try out new styles.

A note of caution: be wary of asking for feedback from others. Oftentimes well-meaning critics will end up curtailing your creativity. Conversely, if readers are noticing problems with your style, pay attention and see what you can learn from their criticism (which, I hope, is kind and encouraging).

Be Specific about Your Tone

Part of fine-tuning your writing style to be specific is to make sure it carries the proper tone throughout your book. What is tone?

Tone is a subtle thing, and it overlaps sound, style, and voice. Whereas voice is really generated and inspired by your characters, tone is something more consistent and covers your whole book. It's the overall *feel* you give the narrative and story, regardless of whether you use first-person or third-person POV.

Give a Feel for How You Feel

Tone really has nothing to do with how you construct a sentence, paragraph, or even chapter. Think of tone as *your* overall opinion or feeling about your story. Consider the story you are writing—what emotional attitudes come into play? Sarcasm, humor, cynicism, anger, jubilation? If you're telling a story about oppression and cruelty, is it because you feel passionately about this topic and want people to be moved to take a particular stand?

Of course, this doesn't mean your tone should be inciting a riot. What it does mean is your writing style will convey this feeling you have. Your sentences and scenes will have an undercurrent of seriousness, poignancy, or perhaps intensity. In contrast, if you are writing a lighthearted adventure story, your tone may express humor, flippancy, even a bit of obnoxiousness. What you want is to give a feel for how *you* feel.

Tone is subjective, and you do want to be careful your tone doesn't come across haughty, know-it-all, or pompous. It's fine to have a character who is pompous, but you don't want the tone of your novel to be pompous (unless intended, in perhaps a humorous manner). I hope you can see the difference. Your character may speak with purple prose and long-winded sentences, but your overall writing style shouldn't smack of an attempt to use big words and convoluted thinking in an effort to impress readers (who won't be impressed; they'll be annoyed).

Build your sentences influenced by how you feel about this character and the story you are telling. That way the *tone* of that novel will be *your* subjective tone—not the character's. If this character is a dark, evil man who did horrible crimes against humanity, your tone will be serious, intense, maybe even a bit objective to give distance and let the reader feel what she may.

Consider How Much "Author" Presence You Want

Another consideration when being specific in your style is to determine just how much you want your presence as the author to

194

show through. Tom Robbins and John Irving are two authors who make a point of "leaking through" their story narrative in a very present (some might say "invasive") way. That's their chosen style, and it earned them a lot of acclaim.

Take a look at a couple of paragraphs from the beginning of Robbins's 1976 best seller *Even Cowgirls Get the Blues* (italics are mine for emphasis):

> It is not a nose, chin or forehead. It is not a biceps, a triceps or a loop-of-Henle.
>
> It is something else.
>
> It is a thumb. The thumb. The thumbs, both of them. It is her thumbs that we remember; it is her thumbs that have set her apart. It was thumbs that brought her to the clockworks, took her away, brought her back. Of course, it may be a disservice to her, as well as to the Rubber Rose, to emphasize the clockworks—but the clockworks is fresh and *large in the author's mind right now*. The image of the clockworks *has followed the author through these early sentences, tugging at him*, refusing to be snubbed. The image of the clockworks tugs gently at the author's cuff, much as the ghost of Duncan Hines tugs at the linen tablecloths of certain restaurants, little that he can eat now . . .

Tom Robbins is almost a character in his books, by way of insertion.

I'm a big fan of Kurt Vonnegut's writing (*Cat's Cradle* being one of my all-time favorite novels). He had a snarky, wry style that tainted everything that happened in his novels. You get the sense of these authors' opinions and beliefs, and that's intentional.

However, writers who let their personal feelings, opinions, and attitudes come through their prose when it's not appropriate for their genre, premise, or plot are going to run into trouble. Readers will cry "author intrusion!" and that presence thrust into the story will feel invasive and jarring.

So I hope you have a good feel now for what it means to be specific about a writing style.

Concise Writing Is Mostly about Mechanics

To have a strong pillar of novel construction, your writing style also needs to be concise. *Concise* means "brevity of expression or statement; free from all elaboration and superfluous detail," says *Merriam-Webster's Collegiate Dictionary*. Some synonyms are *terse, succinct, laconic, summary, pithy, compendious*. As I often declare: "Say what you mean. Don't say what you don't mean." Choose your words carefully and make them count.

Don't belabor these details in your first draft; just get the writing on the page. But when you begin fine-tuning during your revisions, take the time to cut down clunky writing, choose stronger nouns and verbs, and eliminate repetition. Unless of course you have a *specific* and deliberate reason for being exceptionally wordy and convoluted—such as when having a pompous and self-absorbed character talk endlessly in circles about practically nothing.

Track Down Those Weasel Words

Seek and destroy weasel words. Those are words you throw in there without thinking, usually due to the way you were taught to speak, and you probably know which ones you tend to use (often an editor or critique partner will point them out). I have a long list of weasel words I gravitate toward to excess, and I often do a Find and Replace in Word in my current draft to seek and destroy them.

Some of these you might use excessively: *just, very, began to, started to, rather, up, down* (as in "he stood up and then abruptly sat down," which can usually be written simply as "he stood and then abruptly sat.").

You can also find adverbs (Find *ly*) and weak construction (*it was, there were, ing*) the same way. Changing "she was listening to him as he was relating his story" to "she listened to him while he related his story" is an example of being concise.

Good writers know that adverbs can weaken writing, so a great way to make your writing more concise is to search and find those *ly* words and come up with a better way to show the emotion or action implied. Change "she said angrily" to "she said, with an angry tinge to her voice." Or just show through action she's angry. Don't tell the reader; show it. That's being concise.

One last tip about being concise: don't use what's called "purple prose." That means avoid packing your paragraphs with fancy five-dollar words no one knows. Do you really think your readers want to stop every minute or so and reach for a dictionary? No, they don't. Again, you might have a braggadocio character that is keen on tossing about eight-syllable arcane words that haven't been uttered since the Middle Ages. But that's different from infusing your writing with such words. As the saying goes: "Don't use a five-dollar word when a five-cent word will do."

Take the Time to Learn How to Write Well

This may seem unnecessary to say, but, believe me—it needs to be said. I can't tell you how many novels I edit and critique that show a dearth of basic language composition skills. Many writers can barely construct a complete sentence or a coherent one. Being a great writer requires learning the language you write in. You need to understand basic grammar, punctuation, and word usage. If you misspell a lot of words and put commas in the wrong places and use words incorrectly, your writing will suffer. I wish I didn't need to say all this, but I do.

Learn your craft and wield language adeptly. Words are the tools of your vocation. You are building a story, and as with building anything, you need to know how to handle your tools. If you need to, take classes at a college and buy (and study) some books on grammar. (Try my fun book *Say What?* if you really don't like learning this stuff!) I know, it's like getting a tooth pulled. But in the long run, you'll feel much better. Trust me. Writing will come much easier if you learn how to write correctly.

You don't have to be perfect—that's why you hire an editor to polish and proofread your manuscript. But the more you can do yourself, the less you will have to rely on an editor to do damage control. And it will cost you less in the long run—in money and time.

So, although I've only briefly discussed what concise writing is, I hope you get the gist of it. Have fun developing your unique writing style, tailored to fit your genre, and while you're at it, take time to improve your grammar, punctuation, and word usage. If you aren't sure of a word's meaning, look it up.

Here's your eleventh checklist! Photocopy the checklist or type this link into your Internet browser: http://bit.ly/1wJIPUA. Think about printing out multiple copies to keep in a folder, to access anytime you are working on any novel.

Ready for the last pillar of novel construction? Coming right up.

Inspection Checklist #11
Writing Style—Concise and Specific

Question #1:

Have you gone through your scenes to ensure the characters' narrative voices are different from your "writer's" voice?

Question #2:

What genre are you writing in? Have you studied numerous novels in your genre to "get" the range of writing styles that are appropriate?

Question #3:

Have you done a search through your novel for your weasel words and removed or replaced with stronger words?

Question #4:

Have you done a search for weak construction, such as *ly* and *ing* to find passive voice and adverbs that may be causing clunky writing?

Question #5:

Have you gone through every sentence to make sure you've chosen the best, most appropriate words to convey your intended meaning?

Question #6:

Can you find passages you sense are forced, pretentious, or fake? Try freewriting new passages with simple, honest intent. Any better?

Question #7:

Read through your scenes and pay attention to how your body feels. Do any passages feel "wrong" to you? If so, try rewriting until they feel right.

Question #8:

Do you spend time reading great novels? Who are your favorite authors in your genre? Are you taking time to read to inspire your writing? If not, schedule it!

Question #9:

What type of tone is best for your book? Have you gone through your scenes to bring out that tone through all the narrative?

Question #10:

Have you thought about how much or little you want your "writing voice" to come through your narrative? What's best for your genre?

Question #11:

Do you struggle with grammar, punctuation, and word usage? If so, have you committed to buying some books and/or taking English classes to improve?

Question #12:

Have you given yourself permission to "let yourself go" and experiment with your writing style? If not, be brave and take risks!

Pillar #12: Motifs for Cohesion and Depth

Chapter 26: The Superglue of Novels

Hard to believe we are now about to examine the twelfth and final pillar of construction—motifs. We've taken a long, hard look at what's needed to support a weighty story to this point, and I hope by now you've used the inspection checklists to analyze every aspect of your novel to make sure it's built with solid, enduring materials.

Lots of other little bits can be added into a novel, such as literary devices (allusions and metaphor and the like) and puns and wild humor, but they are the "extras"—similar to the decorative lighting fixtures and ornamental hardware you put on your finished house. So long as you focus first and foremost on getting the foundational structure right—building all twelve pillars before fiddling with the minor elements—you can't go wrong.

Too often I deal with novels that are essentially train wrecks when it comes to structure. Or, in keeping with our construction motif, I should say they are like buildings hastily thrown together by toddlers wielding plastic buckets and shovels in the sandbox. The entire structure is built, in a sense, out of sand. Best to throw a pail of water on the thing and walk away. Often there is little, if anything, that can be salvaged from such a structure.

Keep this in mind when dealing with revision, for if you are toying with the minor elements but disregarding any of these essential pillars, it just might be a big waste of time. And who has time to waste?

Glue and Superglue

So, with that said, let's take a look at our last essential pillar of novel construction. You may wonder why I consider motifs an important element in stories. Surely not every novel in every genre needs to contain a motif (or two or five), but motifs can supercharge your story, and it's very likely that if you add some, you can make your novel more interesting and memorable. I noted earlier that theme is the glue that binds the elements of your novel. Well, motifs are like Superglue. A little goes a long way.

Motifs can make the difference between an okay story and a terrific one. Novels that present powerful motifs reach readers on multiple levels, for we humans resonate with symbols, and although a motif isn't strictly (or always) a symbol of some sort, a motif carries symbolic import to some extent.

Symbolism Is at the Heart of Culture

Cultures from the dawn of time have utilized symbols, and in many cultures these symbols are not only foundational, they contain deep meaning and often are used to instruct and define their society. I don't mean to go into a history lesson, for I'm sure you understand what I'm talking about. Motifs and symbols, in other words, can reach us on deep, primal, unconscious levels.

Is that a good thing? I believe it is. If you've read *Writing the Heart of Your Story* (one of the books in The Writer's Toolbox series), you know I'm all about reaching not just the heart of your story but your own heart and the heart of the reader. To me, a novel is a bridge from one heart to another—the writer's to the reader's. Motifs are an element you can use in constructing your novel that can create that bridge.

The Difference between Motif and Theme

Let's first make the distinction between theme and motif, since we've already looked at what theme is and its importance in your novel. You may have a number of themes weaving through your story that also work to tie all your elements together.

Your novel may explore themes like bigotry, greed, revenge, or forgiveness, and the plot and characters embody and showcase these themes to get across your "take-home" message for your book (if you have one). Remember: theme is what your book is "really about." But a theme is not a motif.

Merriam-Webster's defines *motif* this way: "A usually recurring salient thematic element (as in the arts); especially a dominant idea or central theme." For our purposes, for ease of understanding and application, I prefer to leave theme out of this definition, treating it as a separate entity altogether. But the key to *motif* is in these two words: *recurring* and *salient*. (*Salient* meaning something that juts out, rises above, projects significantly or conspicuously.)

Motifs are symbolic elements packed with inference. Motifs can be a "thing"—some object that makes a repeated appearance in your novel. Or they can be word or phrase, a concept, an image—just about anything that can be repeated with significance and symbolism. The weather can be a motif, for example, if each time something terrible is about to happen, "lightning" strikes.

Image Systems for Your Novels

In my book *Shoot Your Novel* I speak at length about image systems that filmmakers utilize to give this kind of depth and cohesion to a film. Without reiterating too much, an image system comprises specific images, colors, phrases, symbols—essentially motifs—among many other things. Books like *The Bluest Eye* (Toni Morrison) and *Riders of the Purple Sage* (Zane Grey) used a specific color repeatedly as a motif (not hard to guess which color, right?). Bringing your motif into your title, as you can see, adds that powerful cohesion to the story.

I mention various movies that bring motifs into play, such as the element of water in *What Lies Beneath*, the play and detail of light in *K-Pax*, and the fairy tale elements in *The Silence of the Lambs*. Great storytellers will spend time thinking of motifs they can infuse into their story to give it greater depth.

Repetition Is the Key

Repetition, as we all know, is what helps us remember. My psychology professor in college said that if you repeat something (like a person's name) aloud seven times in a short amount of time (such as in one conversation), that word or phrase will transfer from the part of the brain that stores short-term memory to the part that stores long-term memory (or something like that. I learned this a lot of years ago and, sadly, I did not repeat his exact words seven times aloud to ensure I remembered it correctly!).

But I hope you get my point here. If you use a motif in your book repeatedly, readers are going to notice, and when they recall your book months later, often those motifs will be the main things they do remember. At least that's how I am. When I think of Leif Enger's novel *Peace Like a River*, the first thing that comes to mind is the repeated phrase that serves as a powerful motif in his story—his character young Reuben Land saying, essentially, "This is what I saw. This is what I heard. Make of it what you will."

In *To Kill a Mockingbird* the motif of birds is reiterated in not just words but conceptually. A bird is used in the title, drawn from a key line in the story that serves as the theme—about mockingbirds being harmless and so shouldn't be harmed. In addition, the key character's name is Finch—which is the name of a very small bird (which might seem to be incapable of putting up a big fight against a huge, vicious bird [read: racism]).

The mockingbird is a symbol that glues Harper Lee's story together, just as the *mockingjay* is a symbol used very literally in *The Hunger Games*—as the main character, Katniss, uses the call of the mockingjay, and is given a mockingjay pin to wear, which has rebellion written all over it. Even the trailers for the movies use the short mockingjay whistle-call as an identifier for the films.

How many of us repeated the musical pattern that was a key element in communicating with aliens in *Close Encounters of the Third Kind*? I still can hum it after decades. Why? Because it was used as a motif repeatedly through the movie (and is a main element of the plot). Sorry if I reminded you about this—it will probably now be stuck in your head for days.

So you can see that a motif can be many things, even a few musical notes. Although it's probably not going to be all that effective to describe a musical ditty in your novel, you have plenty of other ways to present motifs.

Do you see how powerful a motif is? Do you want readers to remember your novel years—maybe even decades—from now? One way (in addition to writing a terrific story that has all the other eleven pillars constructed well) is to use motifs.

How to Come Up with Motifs in Your Novel

Motifs are powerful elements that writers can take advantage of when constructing their novels. But few novelists ever give thought to adding motifs. They might do so subconsciously or inadvertently, but I'd like to encourage you to take some time and deliberately construct some motifs so that they serve as Superglue in your story.

The best way to bring a motif into your story is to tie it intrinsically into your theme. In *To Kill a Mockingbird*, the themes surrounding racism, justice, mercy, and compassion are symbolized by the motif of the harmless mockingbird.

They first appear when Jem and Scout are learning how to use their new rifles. Atticus won't teach them how to shoot, but he does give them one rule to follow: "I'd rather you shot at tin cans in the back yard, but I know you'll go after birds. Shoot all the blue jays you want, if you can hit 'em, but remember it's a sin to kill a mockingbird."

Scout, the narrator, goes on to say:

> That was the only time I ever heard Atticus say it was a sin to do something, and I asked Miss Maudie about it.
>
> "Your father's right," she said. "Mockingbirds don't do one thing but make music for us to enjoy. They don't eat up people's gardens, don't nest in corncribs, they don't do one thing but sing their hearts out for us. That's why it's a sin to kill a mockingbird."

The topic of mockingbirds turns up once more in the book, when Scout is telling Atticus she understands about not dragging Boo into court.

> Atticus looked like he needed cheering up. I ran to him and hugged him and kissed him with all my might. "Yes sir, I understand," I reassured him. "Mr. Tate was right."
>
> Atticus disengaged himself and looked at me. "What do you mean?"
>
> "Well, it'd be sort of like shootin' a mockingbird, wouldn't it?"

All Boo Radley does is watch the neighborhood and leave trinkets for Jem and Scout. Like killing a mockingbird, arresting Boo for coming out of hiding and protecting the children when attacked would serve no useful purpose, and would harm someone who never meant anyone any harm. So over the course of the novel, killing mockingbirds is associated with the sinful, the pointless, and the cruel. This is a great example of using an object or thing (a specific kind of bird) as a motif to amplify themes. You can do likewise in your novel.

Generating Ideas for Motifs

Once you work to develop the themes in your novel, you can create some motifs. Think for a moment about your theme, what your story is *really* about. What images come to mind that might represent your novel? When creating an image system, one thing that might help is to envision a movie poster for your story.

Ask: What key moment in your entire story would best be shown on your poster? What colors and objects would be shown? What would the characters be wearing, holding, doing? By imagining this movie poster, you might get some ideas for strong symbols that you can work into your novel, even if you've already written your first draft. The great thing about motifs is you can add them in after you think you're done with your novel.

Come Up with an Object

Think about your protagonist. Imagine one object she owns that is special to her. Maybe it's a gift someone gave her that has great significance. Maybe it's a shell she found on the beach on an important day in her life. You can find a place to introduce this motif-object early on in the book, then show it again a few times at important moments in your story, and then bring it into the final scene in some symbolic way. All your character may have to do is pick up the shell from off the table and look at it and think about it. She might perhaps recall the pivotal day she found it, and how she felt back then, and how she's changed since then. That is a very effective use of a motif.

Objects can spur not just memory but powerful emotion, so if you have an object connected to a very important moment in a character's past (whether something painful or joyful), you can then springboard from there to infuse this object with deep meaning. Do you still have that dried flower you pressed between the pages of a book years ago from that boy who broke your heart? A ticket stub to that rockin' concert you attended or the movie you saw on your first date with the first guy or gal you had a crush on? We often treasure keepsakes. We *keep* something for the *sake* of remembering. Using a keepsake for a motif can have powerful emotional impact.

Move from Object to Concept

To take it further using the shell as an example, you could have multiple connections with this object, so that not just the shell itself is a symbol or triggers a memory. Perhaps a concept can be formed around the object and brought out. What can a shell represent? Maybe you choose a barnacle that clings tenaciously to a rock to survive, but the harsh waves have broken it free from the rock, and now the creature inside is dead. If you have a character whose life has been shattered by a horrific event, and she's now lost and floundering, dying inside, that shell can take on heavy symbolism.

What if you choose a sand dollar (I use one in my novel *Someone to Blame* as a motif), which is sometimes thought of as a symbol of hope, or to represent redemption, salvation, or restoration of faith? Or you could choose an oyster, which creates a beautiful pearl due to a speck of sand irritating its tender flesh. If your character can "relate" in some way to this shell—if it can reflect or represent something significant to her—you have a powerful motif. An oyster is pretty ugly to look at, but inside a thing of beauty is created out of pain. Right there can be found a lot of symbolism for a variety of story types.

Reinforce the Motif

Take that last idea one step further. If a character feels ugly, unworthy of love, and then is given a string of pearls by the man who comes to love her, this reinforces the motif.

A client of mine had a weak title for her novel, and also needed something to superglue her story to take it to a higher level. She has an early scene showing her main character, a young Russian girl, who is given a cheap bracelet by her drunk mother's unfaithful lover. Angry at her pathetic lot in life, this girl throws down the bracelet and breaks the links of the chain. Her life at this point is shattered. By adding a scene near the end of the book showing her adoptive mother in the US giving her a fine quality link bracelet to represent the mother's love for her new daughter, the symbolism is brought out. The original weak title was changed to *Scattered Links* (author Michelle Weidenbenner), in

208

order to drive home this motif of the bracelet and the links. The word *link* also becomes charged due to its association with the character being linked to new family members and friends, and breaking and repairing the links to her past. As a result, this good novel became a great one, and went on to win some prestigious awards.

So spend some time thinking about your protagonist. What is her biggest emotional issue? What is the lie she believes about herself and can't get past? What is her core need? Can you brainstorm a list of ten or so items in her life or past that could be symbolic for her?

Freewriting and Word Association

One thing you can do is a word-association exercise. Write down an emotion or thematic component from your novel, such as grief or forgiveness. Then freewrite all the words and images that come to your mind without censoring what you write. Picture in your head your character grieving. Where is she? What does she see? What does she touch or hold? What comforts her—a song, a picture, a place?

Go over your list and see if you can grab two or three of these items and find ways to give them a place in some scenes. Perhaps your character can find this object. Or sees it in a store window. The possibilities are endless, but the key to all this is 1) it must have emotional significance for the character 2) it should somehow tie in with your themes, and 3) it should be simple and clear in its symbolism.

Let's say you have freedom as an important theme. You may have chosen "bird" as one of the words that came to mind when freewriting. A bird is a common symbol for freedom and, hence, a good one (using universal symbols that many people share is a good thing). A caged bird represents imprisonment (on any level—actual, emotional, etc.).

Do you remember the best seller *Jonathan Livingston Seagull?* I thought it was pretty corny, but it sold more than a million copies and topped the *New York Times* best-seller list for thirty-eight weeks. It was even made into a movie. The novella featured a seagull named Jonathan (who knows why—perhaps to symbolize the "ordinary man") who is a member of a flock in which individuality is frowned upon. Jonathan finds himself a loner and an outcast. After performing feats of tremendous courage and skill, he is expelled from the flock. This gives him the freedom to develop his skills, and in so doing he reaches a heaven of sorts. The lessons that Jonathan learns in his travels reflect both a greater peace of mind and a freedom to be himself.

Although this book was an allegory (and a bit over-the-top preachy, to me—but hey, that was the '70s!), featuring a young seagull's efforts to rise above the ordinary, it can teach us something about the power of motifs and symbols.

You don't have to go whole-hog into allegory to make powerful points in your novels, however. Just using a few well-developed and meaningful motifs can add that cohesion and depth your novel might be lacking. Why not give it a try?

Layering Motifs in Your Novel for Depth

When our beach house fell off a cliff due to El Nino years ago, we felt a horrible sense of loss at this sudden catastrophe. We had been married on the back deck, and the spot we'd stood upon and said our vows now hung out sixty feet in the air, a hundred feet above the roaring surf. In combing the beach after the disaster, I picked up one brick from the fireplace that we'd spent many long, peaceful hours in front of, watching the crackling fire and listening to the pounding surf.

I kept that brick on my kitchen window sill for years, and you can imagine the symbolism it held for me—and not just reminding me of my loss. For it also symbolized for me that something solid was salvaged from the wreck of my house (and of my family, which suffered massive emotional destruction). Seeing it gave me resolve, comfort, and inspiration.

Objects in your novels can do likewise for your characters when you tie them in with key events in their past.

So you can start, perhaps, with an object that serves as a key motif in your story, then try to take it further. Explore this object in your mind and see what ideas it sparks. Play with those word associations. Think of emotional associations you can generate for this object (for your character) that will serve your plot and your character's goal. What kind of object can symbolize persistence for him? Or represent an obstacle? What note would your character write and stick on his fridge to keep him going?

Secondary Characters Can Introduce a Motif

I try to come up with at least four or five motifs for every novel I write. I think of an object or two to work with, as well as a few key words or phrases that I have characters repeat either in speech or in their heads or both. Often a secondary character who serves as an ally to the protagonist will be the one to impart words of wisdom and advice, and this is a good opportunity to come up with a special phrase (and if possible, one associated with some object) that can then be an important motivator for the protagonist.

In my sweet historical Western romance *Colorado Promise* (written under my pen name Charlene Whitman), I had a minor character tell my protagonist that people in their town had a saying: "Bloom where you're planted." (I found this fact via my research, and it was perfect for the motif I had in mind for my book). Since I had my botany-loving heroine take out west a special plant she loved, I repeated the motif and symbolism of both the plant (object) and the concept (growth, thriving, withering, adaptation) in various scenes, including the last wrap-up scene, which shows her finally planting the small tree in Colorado soil so it can "bloom where it's planted." This motif was factored in before I began writing, and its use was carefully placed.

So think about a secondary ally character that can give advice or insight in a way that will introduce or reinforce a motif in your story. Maybe even come up with a clever phrase for that character to use as a word whisker that serves as a motif.

Motifs Add Richness to Characters

In my novel *Intended for Harm*, I gave each of my seven main POV characters a motif. Each character was developed around a natural element. Jake was wood, Leah was water, Reuben was rock, Simon was fire, Levi was metal, Dinah was air, and so on. From this idea came multiple levels of motifs. Simon had a fiery temper. He smoked all the time when a teenager. He embodied anger due to the specific hurt and rejection he suffered. He set the bed on fire. Reuben, the firstborn son, was the rock of the family. He loved to rock climb. He was also the big obstacle (rock) in the way for his mother. I had a great time playing one element off another. For, Leah (water) was the only one who could calm Simon and take the fire out of him, whereas Simon's "fire" kept setting his father (wood) aflame with anger.

This may seem way over the top, but to me, using these elements as rich motifs and symbols helped me write what I feel is my best novel. These elements, please note, were not randomly chosen. They inspired some of the characters' traits, but they worked purposefully in my story. Otherwise I wouldn't have used them. So don't choose random objects or words for motifs just because they're catchy or unusual. Motifs need to serve the interests of the plot and tie in carefully with your themes.

Think about your characters and their personalities. Is there an object that can emphasize a key trait? Give insight into your character? Something he looks at or holds that keeps him going, keeps him plodding despite pain and opposition to his goal?

If you take the time to bring these motifs into your story, you won't regret it. Your plot might not necessitate a motif, but I highly encourage you to consider building this pillar of novel construction. If done well, it can only help to make your novel more solid, substantial, and memorable.

One last suggestion regarding motifs: I always try to find a way to bring the motif (especially if it's a line some character thinks or says) into the last scene of the novel, and particularly close to the last page. This drives home the motif and helps to give a wonderful satisfying sense of closure and coming full circle in a story. It provides that lingering aftertaste that stays with the reader long after she closes the book (or turns off her e-reader).

Believe it or not, we've now covered all twelve key pillars of novel construction! You have all your inspection checklists. Print them out and use them to closely examine your novel structure. If you can answer all 144 sets of questions to your satisfaction (and be hard on yourself!), your novel will bear the weight of scrutiny.

Photocopy the checklist or type this link into your Internet browser: http://bit.ly/1GzVZXn.

Inspection Checklist #12
Motifs for Cohesion and Depth

Question #1:

What are three-four motifs you can come up with for your novel that will tie in with your theme? Describe them.

Sword, horse, plus!

Question #2:

Can you think of an object/item from your protagonist's past that is emotionally charged? Use that for a motif repeatedly.

Question #3:

Can you think of a symbol that has some universal (or common) meaning that can become significant for your protagonist? Put it in.

Question #4:

Have you created an image system for your novel? Describe it, and include words, colors, phrases, objects. Bring them into your story.

Question #5:

Picture your movie poster for your novel. What important objects and setting stand out? Create motifs from those.

Question #6:

Think of the main emotion or trait your protagonist experiences (grief, forgiveness, etc.) Can you find a symbol/object for this to use in your novel?

Question #7:

Can you think of a phrase or sentences an ally character can say to your protagonist that can be repeated as motif?

Question #8:

Consider the title of your novel. Can you find a way to bring a motif into the title? Tie in with your themes?

Question #9:

Think of the main themes of your story, then freewrite word associations of emotions, objects, or images. Can you use some of these for motifs in your story?

Question #10:

What comforts your character the most? A song, phrase, object, person? Find a way to use as a motif in your book.

Question #11:

Pick the three most important scenes in your novel for your protagonist. Can you insert the same motif into those three scenes somehow?

Question #12:

When your novel is done, what motif can you bring out in both the first scene and the last (with your protagonist) that features your main motif?

Part 3: Brainstorming and Mind Mapping Your Pillars of Construction

Chapter 27: Brainstorming to Build Strong Pillars

We've spent a lot of time examining the twelve pillars of novel construction, and I hope you've gained a lot of great, new insights on how to "build" a novel. You now have a toolbox full of handy building tools, as well as a handle on how to use them. The twelve pillars we've looked at are foundational to your story; they hold it up. If any of these pillars are weak, your novel will fail. It's as simple as that.

I spoke early on about approaching the writing of a novel in a holistic manner rather than piecemeal. In other words, there is a big problem in tackling a huge undertaking such as a novel by looking at the pieces as separate components that can be developed apart from all the others.

A Novel Is Not a Sum Total of Its Parts

Many writing craft books teach this piecemeal approach. They discuss how to write a good plot, or how to come up with tight dialog, or how to create interesting characters. Yes, all these components are part of a novel. But just because there are twenty-six letters in the English language, that doesn't mean you can combine them any which way and end up with the greatest novel of the century. Novels, like houses or skyscrapers or jet planes, must have all their parts working together smoothly and for one ultimate purpose—to perform in the manner intended.

When you begin to kick around ideas for a novel, it's like rummaging through a barrel of mechanical parts. You might pull out a few dozen nuts, bolts, wires, spark plugs, and metal plates. You might know the many uses for each part, and if you took the time, you could craft some cool-looking sculptures. Maybe even something functional. In junior high, I learned how to wire a Masonite board so that if I touched two wires together, a lightbulb lit up (I thought I was pretty clever).

But we writers don't want to just throw a bunch of parts together and hope we end up with a neat-looking novel. We want a novel that holds together on every level. This is the biggest problem, hands down, that I see in the hundreds of novels I critique every year. Most of them are like these creative building projects. There seems to be some idea or theme or purpose to them, something hinted at, but when I stand back (or stare up close), I can't see the forest for the trees. There are a lot of trees, some very pretty, but no forest. No true, clear, compelling, powerful story.

What I'm saying is a novel is not a sum total of all its parts. Not by a long stretch. This is why I've emphasized spending time brainstorming and mind mapping your plot, characters, setting, themes—all your elements. And why I urged you to work on all the key corner support pillars of your novel together until all four are tightly knit.

The Perils of Working Piecemeal

Let me elaborate. I see a lot of novels that have a great premise or plot idea. They might even have a terrific Concept with a Kicker. But . . . there isn't a clear protagonist. I have no clue *who* the story is about (for a novel must be about someone!). Or I may see there's a protagonist, but most of the time, she has no goal, ever, in the book. I keep waiting, waiting, waiting . . . and by the end of the book, I shake my head. What did that character want? Why were they even in the story? Oh, so the plot could be shown. Ugh.

And then, there are novels with a great concept and a protagonist with a terrific goal, but there is zilch tension and the pacing drags and the book is torturous to read to the end. Why? Because there are no stakes. No central conflict. You can have a character with a "lofty" goal of wanting to climb Mt. Everest. Maybe he's a really intriguing character—funny, original, empathetic. But the book contains little to no conflict. Of course, climbing Everest has inherent high stakes—our hero could lose his life, and that risk brings tension with it. And maybe there's a snowstorm or an accident, but overall there is no *central* conflict or specific inner conflict based on a deep core need. And

218

without that, the book reads like a string of events, ups and downs, with no real purpose to it. Which brings me to . . .

Theme. For theme is the glue that binds those three elements: the Concept with a Kicker, the Protagonist with a Goal, and the Conflict with High Stakes. Theme is the heart of your story, and it speaks of the heart of your protagonist, who must embody the theme. If your protagonist's goal for that novel is *only* to get to the top of Everest, that isn't going to ensure the book will be riveting. It might be a great novel if it has amazing writing and interesting characters who engage in clever dialog, with some conflict. But even with all that, if there isn't a *point* to the story, it will fall a bit flat. It may get some nice reviews and garner some readers who really enjoyed the book. But it could be so much better, so much more, if themes were developed that wove through the novel and were intrinsic to the character's core need.

Join All Those Components Together

This is what I mean by holistic. Working all the pillars together, as if using fasteners between posts in a building to add additional sturdiness. When we built our bed and breakfast on a cliff overlooking the rugged north coast back in 1989 in California, we made it through plan check just fine—until the county building department decided we needed to add additional support for earthquake safety. That meant an added cost of nearly twenty thousand dollars in metal struts and fasteners to bolt to the posts and studs throughout. When the building was completed, our contractor shook his head and said, "Well, now you could bulldoze this building off the cliff and it would crash on the beach two hundred feet below and stay in one piece."

Were we glad we had to cough up that much money for a bunch of metal strips and bolts? No—but we changed our tune when over the next ten years we got hit with some big earthquakes—including two that destroyed sections of nearby towns and freeways (we were on the biggest earthquake fault in California). Our inn remained unscathed. I think we sustained a few hairline cracks in a ceiling or two. But that's all.

Wouldn't it be nice if, after you finish writing your novel and publish it, you only got an occasional "hairline" crack (read: negative review)? If you make sure all your pillars of novel support are strong, you can be sure your novel will hold up.

Brainstorming Your Pillars

I mentioned early on in this book that I would give you some ideas on how to holistically brainstorm these pillars—and particularly the four essential corner pillars. By using the workbook created to accompany this book, you'll have plenty of prompts and help to delve deeply into brainstorming and mind mapping. But I'll give you a basic overview in this chapter to get you acquainted with practical ways to brainstorm the construction of your novel such that all the pillars mesh together in purposeful intention.

Maneuvering through the Stormy Mess

Anyone who writes at some point has to brainstorm. We start with an idea or something as simple as an image, and from there, pushed by the desire to morph that idea into something bigger, we come up with other ideas that start linking together. And whether we conceive of these ideas in a logical fashion or more of a stormy mess, there is some sort of process whereby we move from initial concept to a creative work. Whether we are writing a short blog post or magazine article or a full-length novel, at some point we have to brainstorm.

In dealing with hundreds of editing clients, I notice that this phase of the creative process related to writing seems to be the most challenging, nebulous, and frustrating for writers. Some of us writers are fortunate to have friends and/or family members who help us kick around ideas and get our creative juices flowing and problem-solve plot points. But most of us often (and sometimes by choice) ideate on our own, in the confines of our lonely office or in a quiet cubicle in the library.

We Often Dread the Process

Needless to say, creativity isn't something that we can just turn on full force, like a water spigot. Oh how we wish we could. It seems some people are just bursting with ideas and can't get them all down fast enough on paper. They seem to be able to convert those bits of ideas into full-fledged concepts and detailed plots without much effort. But most of us don't find this process so easy.

Often I give detailed instructions to my struggling writing clients on how to brainstorm ideas for scenes and characters. They seem intimidated by the whole idea of brainstorming, afraid they will not come up with anything good. Instead of seeing that stage of the writing process as fun and exciting, they dread and avoid it.

Sure, it's puzzling and frustrating at times to rack your brain trying to jiggle loose some good ideas. Sometimes you feel as if you are banging your head against a wall, but to no avail. No solid ideas fall through the cracks.

Through writing more than a dozen novels, I've experimented with various techniques to help me brainstorm ideas. Some work better for me than others, such as writing all my scenes on index cards. But before I can get to the index card stage, I still have to move from random bits of ideas to full-fledged scenes. I've found the very best way to generate and organize these ideas is to use mind mapping. And this is the best way to work on those four corner pillars in a holistic manner.

A Different Kind of Map

Just what is a mind map? Mind maps are much like a travel map, although a bit chaotic at first glance. A mind map is created on a piece of paper or tagboard to capture and connect ideas so your brain has help in moving from the idea stage to the execution stage. This is the place we writers often have the hardest time in our creative process, for it's here where we shift from pure inspiration to the nuts and bolts of logical organization and planning. So mind maps act as a bridge to get you across that daunting chasm.

Ways a Mind Map Can Help Your Writing Process

One great benefit of mind mapping is it can help you quickly identify and understand the structure of a subject or theme. Mind maps help you see the way that pieces of information fit together, and help you remember information, as they hold it in a format that your mind finds easy to recall and quick to review.

Instead of writing pages of notes, mind mapping is a way of word/idea associating that helps generate new ideas. Reading through pages of notes can be tedious and doesn't often aid us in organizing those ideas.

When I brainstorm my novels, I write pages and pages of notes, as freewriting is a method that really works for me in drawing out new ideas, characters, and themes for my stories. However, if I just stopped at writing notes, I would be really stuck as to how to proceed. It's very hard to go from pages of notes to jumping in and writing a novel straight through, so there are mind mapping techniques—visual and tactile aids—that help me create that bridge from idea to execution.

Manageable Chunks

When you mind map, you use one piece of paper (for each specific map). You break large projects or topics down into manageable chunks so that you can plan effectively without getting overwhelmed or forgetting something important. By creating a "shape" of your ideas on one piece of paper, you find it easier to remember the components, which will aid you when you get down to actually writing. You can use a mind map when brainstorming ideas, to summarize info and notes, consolidate info from different sources, to think through problems, and to study and memorize info.

How to Draw a Mind Map

- Write the title of the subject (or a key idea) you're exploring in the center of the page, and draw a circle around it.

- As you come across major subdivisions or subheadings of the topic (or important facts that relate to the subject) draw lines out from this circle, like the beginnings of a spiderweb. Label these lines with these subdivisions or subheadings.

- As you "burrow" into the subject and uncover another level of information (further subheadings or individual facts) belonging to the subheadings, draw these as lines linked to the subheading lines.

- Then, for individual facts or ideas, draw lines out from the appropriate heading line and label them.

- As you come across new information, link it in to the mind map appropriately.

A complete mind map may have main topic lines radiating in all directions from the center. Subtopics and facts will branch off these, like branches and twigs from the trunk of a tree. You don't need to worry about the structure you produce, as this will evolve of its own accord.

Software tools are available if you want to do this the techy way. Bubbl.us, MindGenius, iMindMap, or Mindjet can improve the process by helping you to produce high quality mind maps, which you can then easily edit or redraft.

Using Mind Maps Effectively

Once you start playing with mind mapping, no doubt you'll come up with methods and variations that work for you. Here are some tips:

- *Start with a big piece of paper,* but preferably a large piece of tagboard.

- *Use single words or simple phrases.* Single strong words and short, meaningful phrases can convey the same meaning more potently. Excess words just clutter the mind map.

- *Use color* to separate different ideas. Colors help you to visualize the mind map for recall and can help to show the organization of the subject. I use different colors for each character when brainstorming scene ideas, to indicate whose POV the scene will be in.

- *Use symbols and images.* Pictures can help you to remember information more effectively than words, so where a symbol or picture means something to you, use it. You can cut out pictures from magazines or do Google searches for images and print out pictures that you can then tape onto your chart (or use a glue stick).

- *Use cross-linkages.* Information in one part of a mind map may relate to another part. Here you can draw lines to show the cross-linkages. This helps you to see how one part of the subject affects another.

I find getting back into "kindergarten mode" is creatively stimulating. Don't be afraid to pull out the colored pens, sticky notes, or crayons. Let your right brain have some room to play, and you may be surprised to see how much easier those ideas will flow. Using this technique of mind mapping might be just the thing to help you transform your random bits of ideas into coherent concepts that will give you firm direction on how to move forward to executing a great piece of writing.

Mind Map on the Macro and Micro Levels

I've never seen anyone specifically focus on novel structure or fiction plotting via mind mapping, so I'm going to show you ways I feel mind mapping can be useful for the novelist, and especially in structuring your pillars. The beauty of this technique is in its versatility. You can work on your novel on a macro or micro level. You can create a mind map for every major (and even minor) character, for all your main plots and subplots, and for other aspects such as historical research and setting.

Going deeper, you can merge mind maps, which I'll explain in a bit. But first, let's look at some basic mind maps you can create to help you get your creative juices flowing and bring order to chaos.

Chapter 28: Brainstorming Characters and Theme Together

I'm a character-driven novelist, so I always first start with character ideas along with theme. To use an example, let's take a look at my novel *Someone to Blame*. You can tell by the title what the theme of this novel is. I wanted to explore blame from every angle, and what I had in mind, loosely, was to do a psychological takeoff on Agatha Christie's novel *Murder on the Orient Express*. I had already done a spinoff of her novel *And Then There Were None (Innocent Little Crimes)*, so this novel of hers was on my mind to do next. I had a character, Billy Thurber, whom I wanted to be not my protagonist but the catalyst for exploring this theme of blame. I planned to set the novel in a small coastal town in present day.

So I took out a large piece of paper and wrote "Billy Thurber" in the middle. From there I drew spokes in a circle leading out from his name. I brainstormed various things other characters in the book might blame on a drifter who comes unwanted into a judgmental small town. I asked the question: "Why would someone want to kill or hurt Billy? Because they think he ____" I thought of incidents Billy could be blamed for—theft, fire, blackmail, kidnapping, rape, murder—that would foment jealousy, rage, paranoia, fear. Once I had all these ideas floating around Billy, I started to home in on these incidents and ideas.

I then came up with characters that would embody these different kinds of blame and connected them (using "spokes") with the situations that could develop into plot points for the story. What resulted was a population of diverse members of a community—from a fisherman to a retired couple to a sheriff to a teenage girl desperate for love and affection. I thought: Who could accuse Billy of theft and why? What circumstances could I create to make him look guilty?

All these ideas became spokes connecting to the various ideas on the page. For instance, I came up with a drunk motel owner, bitter over his divorce, looking for trouble, who blames Billy for his motel fire (which he himself sets, hoping to collect the insurance money so he can keep from going under due to his motel repairs and alimony payments).

Remember—You Can Work on These Pillars in Any Order

Since one of the four key pillars is the Protagonist with a Goal, all this work done to generate a strong pillar of theme for my novel had to serve a greater purpose—to lead me to develop my protagonist and her goal for the book. True, this is a bit indirect, starting with theme. But remember what I mentioned early on—you can work on these four corner pillars in any order, switching back and forth and circling around, adding touches and ideas and components until you have the big holistic picture of your four corner pillars.

For me, tackling the theme was my first goal—because it was clearly going to be the focal point of my novel. And now that I had some ideas about theme and all the characters that might help embody my theme, I had little trouble coming up with my protagonist—Irene, a mother of three whose two teenage boys had recently tragically died. All the characters I came up with *blamed someone else* for something. But I wanted Irene—and her husband Matt—to shine a light on the other side of blame: turning it inward. They would blame themselves for their sons' deaths.

So now I had all this blame showcased, but I needed a Concept with a Kicker, so I brainstormed all the various ideas that came to mind until I found the one I wanted. And with this concept I brainstormed all the stakes and risks and consequences I could come up with. I would have Irene feel drawn to this drifter Billy. She would take a stand with him, against the community. Against her husband. By standing alongside Billy—and stepping in to prevent his murder—I had her risk everything precious to her: her family, her job and standing in the community, and yes, even her life. High stakes, showing a passion for her goal—which was not only to heal and save the pained remnants of her family but to save Billy Thurber as well. And not just physically but emotionally and spiritually.

All this came as a result of brainstorming those four corner pillars. Once I had all four solidly in place, I used mind mapping to come up with my settings and plot and subplots—all the other pillars of novel support.

Focusing on Theme in Your Mind Map

I believe the key to brainstorming a strong plot is to explore the themes you want to bring out in your novel. Your characters embody the themes, and you want some character or characters to take one side of an issue and other characters to take an opposing side.

For example, If you're writing a novel that explores the death penalty, think about mind mapping that theme and all the various opinions—pro and con—on the issue. Think of the kinds of characters that might embody each opinion, and give them a valid reason for it. Ask those "why" questions.

Then, on the map you are creating, make notes alongside each character with ideas about their background and personal history that contribute to that deep-seated belief they have about capital punishment. Maybe one character had a friend who was wrongly accused of murder and was found innocent after years of serving time in prison or even being executed. Maybe another character's child was brutally murdered, and the murderer is now free due to some legal loophole.

Remember: passion is at the core of great characters. By giving all your primary characters some hurtful incident in their past or a painful upbringing that makes them passionate about particular thematic issues, their passion will create great conflict. Characters who sit around talking about things they barely care about will not generate conflict—and will put your reader to sleep.

I hope you can see how characters—and particularly your protagonist—should be created and grow organically around the premise and themes of the novel you are writing. You can start either with the theme in the middle of the map, or your protagonist, who will take a stance regarding the thematic elements.

When You're Not Sure What Your Themes Are

If your novel isn't heavy on theme, or you're not sure yet just what themes will arise , write your short concept sentence or idea in the middle, like this: A man finds a note in a bottle that washed up on a beach, which leads to him finding the love of his life. Okay, that's a simple plot concept or idea. You know you want to write a romance, so what themes might come through the story line?

Again, draw spokes outward from your premise and brainstorm ideas of theme that could lead to character development. Ask those important questions about core need and deepest fear. What is that man afraid of? Maybe he's afraid of love. Why? Because his wife died a few years ago, and he doesn't think he will ever be able to love again. Here's a theme about being able to love again after pain and loss.

Maybe the woman (love interest) sent that note in a bottle because she was about to kill herself and wanted to tell someone about her pain. What's her pain? Brainstorm that. Where could she be located and what would she be doing that would make it the perfect setting for her to put a note in a bottle?

You may end up with a lot of stupid ideas that don't work, but by doing this creative mind mapping, you will ultimately come up with some good ones. Let your creativity run amok, and don't censor the ideas you come up with. Have a few laughs over the silly ones, and dig in deeper as you explore the really great ideas.

One Last Point about Characters

Remember, your main character (and hopefully some of your secondary characters) has to grow and change through the novel. At the end, what she's learned showcases your theme. Be sure to generate ideas that relate to this character arc. The spokes connecting to your various characters should include ideas of how your character changes, why she changes, and what things caused her to change. This is important for when you mind map plotting and scenes .

I often work on character arc on a timeline. Sometimes I tape a few pieces of paper end to end and draw a long line horizontally across the middle. At the far left end is the day the novel starts, scene 1. At the far right end is the end. I not only create a parallel line for my protagonist's arc, I create one for all the important secondary characters. I might use sticky notes if the chart is big enough, or I'll write small in pencil, noting first the emotional, spiritual, persona/mind-set of each character when my story begins. I'll then write how they will end up when the story ends. Some characters change for the better, some for the worse. My protagonist should be in her full "essence" by the end of the book, having learned what she needed to learn after making the tough choices that changed her as she faced the obstacles in the story.

You might have only a little of this roughed in when you start writing your novel or when dealing with your finished first draft. But as you delve into your story, seeking a deeper, more meaningful level, you can also deepen these character arcs. But keep in mind that all the changes and growth these secondary characters experience must serve your plot. They must somehow impact your protagonist and his goal and tie in with your themes.

Concept with a Kicker

We've looked at ways to mind map theme and characters, and hopefully you've seen how playing with your theme can help you generate characters. You may want to start with mind mapping your protagonist, for you might already have an idea of a goal for her, and from that pull out your themes.

Remember: most ideas for a novel are just ideas. They are shapeless lumps of clay, so take the time to brainstorm your idea by writing it down on the center of your mind map and generate as many "kickers" as you can. Think of different careers or passions your main character might have. Come up with various settings—and let your imagination fly through both time and locale to see what ideas spark. Consider an assortment of key events in history, or big events you could invent for the purposes of your concept.

Colum McCann's best-selling novel (and 2009 winner of the National Book Award) *Let the Great World Spin* comprises a collection of memorable characters and events surrounding one specific event that occurred on a day in August 1974—when a man stretched a tightrope between the two Trade Towers in New York City and walked across. McCann took a historic event that few people knew about (and maybe cared little about) and fashioned a brilliant story around it. Some of my favorite scenes in the book are the ones showing the tightrope walker preparing for this feat and the grueling discipline and training he underwent (how much of this is true, I have no idea, but my guess is most of this came from the author's imagination).

So as you brainstorm your idea to turn it into a Concept with a Kicker, play around with the myriad components that can give your

story a fresh approach, with the potential for high stakes—
remembering that the stakes are high *if they matter to the protagonist.*

Conflict with High Stakes

Another effective way to start building these corner pillars is to
work first on your concept and conflict. I mention these two together
because I find it's helpful to formulate a great concept by thinking in
terms of stakes. High stakes are at the heart of a great concept; they go
hand in hand.

Remember my idea for *The Menopause Murders*? My Concept with a
Kicker has to do with a woman going through menopause who kills
thirty-five people (one each time she gets a new symptom). Just that
concept alone implies high stakes—especially for anyone crossing her
angry path, right? But for the protagonist, inherent are lots of high
stakes: getting caught and going to jail, getting hurt when she attacks
someone, losing her husband's love and respect, losing her children's
love, losing her job. I haven't yet begun serious brainstorming on this
novel at the present moment, but this is where I'll be starting when I
do—mind mapping all the conflict and high stakes generated by my
concept.

You could also brainstorm theme and conflict, for having
characters take/embody different sides of an issue generates conflict.
But keep in mind that you want *one central source* of conflict usually in a
novel. So write the word *conflict* in the middle of your piece of paper or
in your mind-mapping software program and start adding spokes
outward leading to all the ways your Concept with a Kicker might
generate conflict and determine just what or who might be that key
source of conflict in your novel and why.

Take time really thinking through all these ideas until you are sure
you have exactly the story you want—and one that will hold up. Then
go through the four corner pillars checklists and put all your ideas to
the test. Do they pass inspection? If so, you can move on to the other
eight pillars.

Chapter 29: Plotting Madness

I love plotting. Actually I hate it too. But when I use mind mapping to plot, it eases my anxiety and becomes really fun. Coming up with plot ideas is a great challenge, and is so essential. I shouldn't have to state that the plot is just a vehicle for your four corner pillars, and in particular, your Concept with a Kicker.

Once you have a solid Concept with a Kicker, put that in the middle of your big chart or piece of paper. Keep in mind your protagonist's arc—how she is going to change and grow, what she learns from the things she experiences in this story, and where she is going to end up (literally and spiritually). This is important because the scenes you brainstorm need to provide the situations for that character to grow and change.

Brainstorm Conflict and Complications

Then start thinking of what scenes you need in order to tell the story you have in mind. Don't focus too much on setting, unless that is key to the point of the scene. Brainstorm various scenarios for your characters, keeping in mind that every scene has to have a point to it and serve the interests of the plot. Avoid secondary plot ideas for now; just focus on the main plot and, most importantly, what your protagonist's plot goal is for the book. What obstacles and conflict can you throw in her way?

Think of worse and worse complications. What is the worst thing that can happen to thwart her? Who can betray her? What can she lose that she thought was vital? A friendship or marriage? A business? A child? Keep in mind to make things as bad and messy for your character as possible. By mind mapping all kinds of plot ideas, you will have enough to sort through to get your basic framework set up.

Brainstorm Twists and Reversals

After you have a number of scene ideas with complications and conflict, draw spokes outward from those ideas and think of how you could twist them or create a reversal. A man gets fired from his job—that's a complication in the story. What twists could you attach to that scene idea? What if his getting fired opens the door for something good to happen, like the truth of some corruption coming out with consequences to his antagonist? What if his getting fired pushes his wife over the edge and she leaves him and disappears with his child?

Play with the expected reaction and see if you can turn it into the opposite. What seems a bad thing becomes a good thing. What seems something inconsequential turns out to be horrific. The person least likely to be an enemy turns out to be the hero's nemesis. Or the one who has always opposed him suddenly does something unexpected to help him. With mind mapping, you can come up with lots of different variations, to give you ideas of ways to both complicate and enrich your plot to make it as intriguing and riveting as possible.

Don't Think Linearly

Don't worry about putting anything in order yet. That will come later. Once I have a couple of dozen strong scene ideas, I start transferring them onto index cards. I'll play with the order as I lay them out on my kitchen table. But when you are mind mapping, you don't need to think linearly yet. You just want to throw ideas onto the paper to let your story start gelling. Try to come up with ten strong scenes that will be the pivotal moments in your story. Moments in which your character will change, be forced to make a choice, be pushed into despair. When you brainstorm like this, you won't likely have a lot of nothing scenes in which characters are just sitting around talking, or doing things that really aren't important to propelling the story forward.

Subplots Serve the Main Plot

I highly recommend you create another mind map once you finish with your main plot map. This one will be your subplot mind map. State your plot summary in the middle of the paper. From there, brainstorm ideas of subplots that can help support your plot. What do I mean? This again ties in with your themes.

If you are writing a novel about a woman who is infertile and desperate to have a baby, you could brainstorm subplot ideas and scenes that will have her face this issue head-on. You can have her best friend accidentally get pregnant while engaged in a fleeting relationship and have an abortion, thinking nothing about it. Or you could have that friend be given a baby to foster, assured she will be able to adopt it, only to have the birth mother change her mind. The subplot could involve this young mother having problems in her life, which throw the two characters together with clashing needs. The key is to make your characters clash, so as you brainstorm scene and subplot ideas, think of ways to do this. And of course these types of subplots bring the themes of your novel to the forefront.

Merging Mind Maps: Characters and Settings

You can create a mind map for various settings in your story that are key to your plot. How? By laying out the many mind maps you've already done on character, theme, and plot. No doubt on those mind maps you came up with places or scenarios for your characters. Go further and actually create very specific places to put them in. Keep in mind the time of year and locale of your book. If some scenes take place outdoors in the winter in Alaska, you want to think of settings that perfectly fit the plot. You may have two characters in an argument on a frozen lake that cracks, sending one into icy water and forcing the other to save him. Remember to use setting and weather effectively in your story; you have an untapped mine of potentially great complications when you are deliberate in your choice of locale and/or weather.

Try to keep away from mundane settings. Sure, you might really need a scene in which two characters are sitting drinking coffee. Maybe one time, if you really need that location and they really have to be drinking something. But push yourself to be as imaginative as you can (without being ridiculous). Mind map places you can put your characters in that will reflect the tone of the scene and the mood of your POV character. Setting can be a powerful component of a scene, so don't brush off the idea of mind mapping these settings to exacerbate the conflicts you've set up between characters.

Merging Mind Maps: Subplots and Settings

Another pair of mind maps you can merge are the subplots and setting ones. Let's say you've come up with some subplots, most likely utilizing your secondary characters. The more you can spiderweb your settings into your story, the more cohesion you'll have. Look at your subplot mind map and then consider the one you created for settings for your protagonist. Find ways to get some of your secondary characters in the same locales as your protagonist. Can you have a secondary character utilize some of the same settings as your main character?

Often novels are set in a town or small enough area that allows (requires?) some of the characters to share settings. A story might be generated around a company, and some of the characters work in the same office. Some may attend the same school. Try to think beyond the obvious, though, and find ways to have characters cross paths or meet in order to overlap setting with subplot.

A subplot may involve a mother having to deal with the high school principal regarding her son's delinquency. So one locale would be the high school. Instead of having her meet with another character—say, her best friend who is going through marital issues—at the coffee shop, where you would have them sitting at a table just talking, you could brainstorm reasons for her friend to be at the school, where they could run into each other and talk. What if her friend is in charge of the prom, and she's there decorating the gym? How much more interesting would it be to have the friend fall apart over her marriage in front of a bunch of excited but stunned seniors, while she's standing at the top of a ladder throwing rolls of crepe paper and talking to your protagonist?

When you brainstorm your secondary characters, you want to find ways to connect them to your protagonist. Settings come into play here, for all characters know people through work, social circles, family, and hobbies. Not all novels are going to allow you to interconnect a lot of settings. With an international thriller, your protagonist may be running all over the world (like in Robert Ludlum's

The Bourne Identity), but if you can find ways to link characters to settings, subplots, and theme, you will weave a tight novel.

"Everything Important I Learned in Kindergarten"

I hope this look at brainstorming has created a whirlpool of ideas in your brain. I have found that by letting my imagination explore through mind mapping, I'm able to come up with lots of great ideas without my internal editor dissing my ideas. By putting anything that comes to mind down on paper, and playing with colored pencils or highlighter pens—even drawing little symbols or squiggles to link elements together—you might be very surprised at the things you come up with.

Sometimes the confines of a computer screen put limits on our imagination. I firmly believe we tap into the joy and freedom of expression and creativity when we let ourselves be "kindergartners" again and take the pressure off the expectation of performance. May you have many happy hours creating your mind maps and building your pillars of novel construction the holistic way.

Chapter 30: Now What?

If you've been careful in your construction, what then? Is there any other way to be sure you haven't missed something?

Sure—get a professional critique. Choose an editor who really has a handle on novel construction, preferably someone who has written and successfully published some novels (although that's not necessarily essential).

Keep in mind that line editing (correcting grammar and punctuation) is not the same thing. Just having a content edit, or even a developmental edit that digs deep into your writing, is not the same as having your "big picture" elements examined. I believe *every* novel can benefit from a professional critique—even those of best-selling authors.

A number of successful authors have me edit and critique all their novels. I can honestly say I have yet to come across the perfect novel that has not needed some work, that did not have some problematic areas that needed revisiting, or that lacked some plot issues that needed resolving. I keep waiting for the day that perfect manuscript will cross my desk—one that I won't have to mark up at all. That I can gaze at, open-mouthed in astonishment in the realization that it is perfect, flawless, and ready to publish. I haven't seen it yet. I know mine sure aren't perfect, and that's why I have my trusted author friends critique my books after I write the first draft (friends who will be tough!).

So think about having your work critiqued—before you have it line edited. Don't put pretty icing on a yucky cake. If you really want to be a great novelist and write those books that will stand up under scrutiny and withstand the test of time, be willing to invest money into creating a beautiful product.

To get the very best out of this book and all the instruction provided herein, be sure to pick up *The 12 Key Pillars of Novel Construction Workbook*. This will help you really dive into developing all your pillars and asking the hard questions that will get you thinking about each one. Print out copies of all the checklists and keep them in a folder for easy access. If you get stuck while plotting out your scenes, you can pull out your completed checklists to peruse and remind you of the important aspects of your story. Keep your mind maps in there as well, and look them over from time to time. They'll help you stay on track so you can construct that sturdy, lasting novel.

A Final Word

Working hard in advance to ensure a strong structure does not take the joy out of creativity or curtail a writer in any way. Quite the opposite is true. Within framework is the freedom to be confidently expressive.

One of my favorite movies comes to mind when I think about novel structure: *The Legend of 1900*. This beautiful story stretching over decades tells about a baby born in 1900 on a cruise ship who is abandoned by an unknown mother, is raised by workers on the ship, and learns to play the piano. This amazing prodigy, however, never steps foot off this ship his entire life. He just can't muster the courage to leave, so he spends his life traversing the Atlantic Ocean, playing in the big band and astounding listeners with his musical talent.

One of the greatest scenes in this movie is when this young man, Danny (also known as 1900) tells his best friend, Max, why he just can't leave the ship. He explains the world is too big, that it doesn't have any boundaries; it has no end. He can't live with such vast possibilities. He needed to define his life "between prow and stern." Land was "a ship too big" for him.

Danny says, "The keys are not infinite. You are infinite. And on those keys, the music that you can make is infinite. . . . But if that keyboard had millions of keys . . . if it was infinite, then on that keyboard there is no music you can play."

Within that framework of eighty-eight keys, a pianist can create an limitless number of pieces, beautiful creations of endless variety. The framework isn't a limitation; it's an opportunity. He adds, "It is life."

And so too, within the framework of expected novel structure, any great idea can come to life. The possibilities are infinite for amazing stories.

You just have to build them—one pillar at a time.

There is nothing more satisfying than holding your novel in your hand and being proud of this magnificent story you've built. And you now have the tools to build many, many great novels!

Happy building!

About the Author

C. S. Lakin is a multipublished award-winning novelist and writing coach who loves to help writers find joy and success in their novel-writing journey. She works full-time as a copyeditor (fiction and nonfiction) and critiques about two hundred manuscripts a year. She teaches writing workshops around the country and gives instruction on her award-winning blog Live Write Thrive.

Lakin lives in a small town south of San Francisco, CA, with her husband Lee, a gigantic lab named Coaltrane, and three persnickety cats. She loves to hike and backpack, cook, watch basketball, and spend time with her two daughters and grandson.

Did you find this writing craft book helpful? The best way to thank a writer is to leave a positive, honest review. Be sure to leave a review for this book that will help other writers learn how to construct a solid, enduring story!

Want to become the best novelist you can be?

The Writer's Toolbox series will give you all the tools you need to write terrific, well-structured stories that will stand the test of time and scrutiny.

If you benefited from *The 12 Key Pillars of Novel Construction,* be sure to get the workbook—a step-by-step in-depth guide to help you develop your novel. Includes hundreds of prompts, worksheets, sample mind maps, and exercises to ensure your novel is structured well and will stand up to scrutiny and thrill readers. (Available in paperback.)

Say What? The Fiction Writer's Handy Guide to Grammar, Punctuation, and Word Usage is designed to help writers get a painless grasp on grammar. You can buy it in print or as an ebook. Available in all formats on all online venues.

Writing the Heart of Your Story: The Secret to Crafting an Unforgettable Novel will teach you how to mine the heart of your plot, characters, themes, and so much more. If you want to write a book that targets the heart of readers, you need to know the heart of your story. You can buy it in print or as an ebook. Available in all formats on all online venues.

Shoot Your Novel: Cinematic Techniques to Supercharge Your Writing— an essential writing craft guide that will teach you the art of "show don't tell" using time-tested cinematic technique. In this era of visual media, readers want more than ever to "see" stories unfold before their eyes. By utilizing film technique and adapting the various camera shots into your fiction, your writing will undergo a stunning transformation from "telling" to "showing." You can buy it in print or as an ebook. Available in all formats on all online venues.

Here's an excerpt of *Shoot Your Novel*:

Shoot Your Novel
Cinematic Techniques to Supercharge Your Writing

INTRODUCTION
POINT AND SHOOT

So, a man walks into a bar, accompanied by a large piece of asphalt. He goes up to the bartender and says, "I'll have a whiskey." He nods at his friend and adds, "Oh, and one for the road."

If I told this joke to you and a group of your friends, I'm not sure you'd laugh as much as I'd hope, but one thing I am sure of—you would each have pictured this playing out in your head, and each would have seen a completely different "movie." Maybe you pictured this taking place in a Western saloon, with the man dressed in cowboy boots and wearing a Stetson hat. He probably had a Texan drawl, and maybe was chewing tobacco as he spoke. Maybe one of your friends imagined a Yuppie high-end urban bar, with soft leather upholstery and smelling of expensive Cuban cigar smoke.

However you envisioned this briefly described scene, no doubt your friends "saw" something wholly different in their minds. Here's the point: if you had watched this in a movie on the big screen, you and your friends would have seen the exact same things. You wouldn't be arguing later whether the piece of asphalt was black or gray or the man was wearing that hat or not. The film itself provided all the details for you, leaving little to your imagination.

Tell It Like You See It

With fiction, though, writers are presented with an entirely different situation. The reader reading your novel will only see the specifics if you detail them. And even if you do, it's likely she will still envision many of the scene elements different from what you hoped to convey.

That's not necessarily a bad thing. In fact, leaving out details and allowing the reader to "fill in the blanks" is part of the reader-writer relationship. In a way, a novel becomes much more personal than a movie, a little bit of a "choose your own adventure" quality. Many love novels just for that ability to "put themselves" into the story, whether it be by relating to a protagonist, seeing people we know in the characters

241

presented, or feeling like we are going through the trials and perils presented by the plot.

The challenge and beauty of the artistic palette a writer uses raises numerous questions:

* How much or how little detail do I (or should I) put in my novel in order to help the reader see the story the way I see it? And how much should I leave to the reader's imagination?

* How can I best write each scene so that I "show" the reader what I want him to see?

* How can I write scenes that will give the emotional impact equivalent to what can be conveyed through a film?

The joke I told was short and didn't give much detail. It had no power or punch, no strong feel of action or movement. I doubt you will remember it a month from now. Other than the man walking and talking and nodding, the "scene" was stagnant, with little to stir the imagination or evoke emotion. Maybe your own writing feels this way to you—often—and you don't know what to do to make it better. Maybe you've read a dozen books on the writing craft and have attended countless workshops at writers' conferences and you still can't seem to "get" how to write powerful, evocative scenes that move your readers. Well, if you sometimes feel like strangling, stabbing, or decapitating your novel because of flat, boring, lackluster scenes, you can shoot your novel instead!

Show, Don't Tell—But How?

Sol Stein, in his book *Stein on Writing*, says, "Twentieth-century readers, transformed by film and TV, are used to seeing stories. The reading experience for a twentieth-century reader is increasingly visual. The story is happening in front of his eyes." This is even more true in the twenty-first century. As literary agent and author Donald Maass says in *Writing 21st Century Fiction*: "Make characters do something that readers can visualize."

We've heard it countless times: show, don't tell. Sounds simple, right? Wrong. There are a myriad of choices a writer has to make in order to "show" and not "tell" a scene. Writers are often told they need to show, which in essence means to create visual scenes the reader can "watch" unfold as they read.

But telling a writer to "show" is vague. Just how do you show? How do you transfer the clearly enacted scene playing in your mind to the page in a way that not only gets the reader to see just what you want her to see but also comes across with the emotional impact you intend?

The Shotgun Method

Writers know that if they say "Jane was terrified," that only tells the reader what Jane is feeling; it doesn't show her terrified. So they go on to construct a scene that shows Jane in action and reacting to the thing that inspires fear in her. And somehow in doing so writers hope they will make their reader afraid too. But that's often like using a shotgun approach. You aim at a target from a hundred yards away with a shotgun and hope a few buckshot pellets actually hit the bull's eye. Many writers think if they just "point and shoot" they will hit their target every time. But then, when they get lackluster reviews, or dozens of agent or publisher rejections, they can't figure out what they did wrong, or failed to do. Why is this? Is there some "secret formula" to writing visually impacting scenes every time?

No, not secret. In fact, the method is staring writers in the face; we have all been raised watching thousands of movies and television shows. The style, technique, and methods used in film and TV are so familiar to us, we process them comfortably and even subconsciously. We now expect these elements to appear in the novels we read, to some degree—if not consciously then subconsciously.

Filmmaker Gustav Mercado, in his book *The Filmmaker's Eye*, makes this very observation about movies, stating that cinematic tradition has become standardized in the way the rules of composition are applied to certain camera shots "which over time have linked key moments in a story with the use of particular shots." His "novel" approach, which he claims is new, is to examine the shot as "a deeper and discursive exploration into the fundamental elements of the visual language of cinema." If this has been proven true with camera technique, it stands to reason the same idea would transfer over into writing fiction. If novelists can learn how filmmakers utilize particular camera shots to achieve specific effects, create specific moods, and evoke specific emotions, they have a powerful tool at hand.

We know what makes a great, riveting scene in a movie, and what makes a boring one—at least viscerally. And though our tastes differ, certainly, for the most part we often agree when a scene "works" or doesn't. It either accomplishes what the writer or director has set out to do, or it flops.

So since we have all been (over)exposed to film and its visual way of storytelling, and its influence on society has altered the tastes of fiction readers, it's only logical to take a look at what makes a great movie. Note that we're not looking at plot or premise in this book, for that's an entirely different subject. Instead, we're going to deconstruct movie technique into bite-sized pieces.

Just as your novel comprises a string of scenes that flow together to tell your whole story, so too with movies and television shows. However, you, the novelist, lay out your scenes much differently from the way a screenwriter does. Whereas you might see each of your scenes as integrated, encapsulated moments of time, a movie director sees each scene as a compilation of a number of segments or pieces—a collection of camera shots that are subsequently edited and fit together to create that seamless "moment of time."

Time to Put On a New Hat

So take off your writer hat for a minute and put on a director one—you know, that sun visor you see the director wear as he's looking through the camera eyepiece on the outdoor set of the big studio lot and as he thinks how he's going to shoot the next scene. Have you ever watched a behind-the-scenes look at how a movie is being filmed, or a TV series? I love watching and listening to Peter Jackson in his many videos detailing the filming of both *The Lord of the Rings* and *The Hobbit* feature films. Jackson does a wonderful job showing the kinds of decisions he has to make as he ponders the shooting of a scene in order to get across the impact, mood, details, and key moments he desires in the final cut.

Directors have to plan like this. They can't show up on the set each morning and look at the shooting schedule and just "wing it." A large sum of money is riding on the director doing his homework and knowing exactly what each scene must convey and show to the viewer. Directors decide just how a scene will be shown and what specifically will be focused on. Using the camera, a director can basically "force"

244

viewers to see exactly what he wants them to see. And one goal in doing this is to evoke a particular emotional reaction from them.

Writing Is Not All That Different from Directing

Writers can do the same. They may not be able to paint so specific a picture that every single reader will envision a novel exactly the same—and that's a good thing. In fact, that's what makes reading novels so . . . well, novel. Readers infuse their personalities, backgrounds, fears, and dreams into a book as they read. A character named Tiffany will conjure up a face for me different from the one you picture in your head. In this way, novels are an interactive experience— the reader's imagination interacting with the novelist's.

Yet, writers can also put on their director's hat—and well they should. Remember, readers nowadays want to read books that are more visual, as Stein remarked—scenes that are happening right before their eyes. But few writers are ever shown just how to do this effectively, and that's what this book is about. You don't have to guess anymore how to "show" a scene in a way that's "supercharged." By learning to use camera shots the way a director does, you too can take readers where you want them to go, make them see what you want them to see. Don't leave that up to the reader to decide. Be not just the writer but the director. Filmmaker Gustav Mercado makes a succinct point in his book: "You should not be subservient to the dictates of a technique but make the technique work for the specific needs of your story instead." What a great truth for both novelists and filmmakers.

So get out of your cozy office chair and follow me onto the set where all the great movies are filmed. Get out your writers' toolbox and be prepared to add a whole new layer of tools—camera shots. Once you learn what these are and how to use them in writing fiction, it's more than likely you will never write the same way again—or look at a scene the same way.

And I truly hope so. I hope once you grab these cinematic secrets and supercharge your novel, you will never take that shotgun out again and just "point and shoot." Instead, you will be the director looking at the scene from all angles and making deliberate decisions on which camera angles to use for the greatest impact.

CHAPTER 1: IT'S ALL ABOUT THE ANGLE

Having spent my entire childhood at the feet of my screenwriter mother, I read more TV scripts than books while growing up, as there were piles of them around my mother's office, and I'd often curl up on the couch and read one after school. I also spent many hours on sound stages and on location watching many of her TV episodes being filmed. Okay, I will confess I liked to sit in Peggy Lipton's chair during the shooting of *Mod Squad*, and if we were outside I wore my mirror shades to be in sync with the dynamic threesome I admired (I rarely saw Clarence Williams III ever take his shades off—indoors or outdoors). I spent many hours wandering in and out of sound stages at Fox, MGM, and other studios where my mother, for a time, had an office. I'd sneak into *M.A.S.H* and watch the banter Alan Alda tossed around as he operated on a fake body in the surgery tent, or mosey on over to *Battlestar Gallactica*. I had fun going on location and even spent a week in San Francisco on the set with Rock Hudson (*MacMillan and Wife*), since my stepfather was the director of that episode, and got to watch some cool stunts involving cable cars (no, Rock didn't do his own stunts!).

I say all this to make the point that growing up in a home that centered around writing and directing for television greatly influenced the way I approach storytelling. Ever since I learned the alphabet, I wrote stories. I even pitched my first script idea at age twelve to the producer of *The Girl from U.N.C.L.E.* Do you remember that show? (Okay just so you know, Stephanie Powers starred in it, and Ian Fleming was the consultant on the show and suggested the idea, but it only ran twenty-nine episodes before being canceled for low ratings. Maybe if they had bought my idea and wrote that script, it wouldn't have failed. Hmm, I wonder . . .) I still have my very polite rejection letter—my first of many! It did help that my mother was a staff writer on the show and had "an in." However, they didn't buy my idea. But you can be sure of one thing—even at age twelve I presented my idea to the producer in a way he could easily visualize it as an episode. My young mind was already programmed to write cinematically.

So when I began writing novels decades later (although I promised my mother I would never be a writer, but that's another story), it was only natural for me to construct all my scenes visually, the way I might see them play out on film. In fact, I couldn't imagine writing any differently. I'm not surprised when I continually get comments from readers like, "I could so picture this book as a movie" or "this novel would make a great movie." I believe they say these things not so much because they think my books are brilliant but because I write cinematically. Every scene is structured either consciously or unconsciously with a series of camera shots, so the reader will see the scene play out the way I see it.

I'm very familiar with the camera shots used—and as I mentioned before, you really are too. If you've watched a few TV shows or seen a few movies, you're already familiar with what I'm going to share with you. What you don't yet know, possibly, is how to transcribe what you see on the screen to the words on your pages. So I'm going to deconstruct movie technique by examining the camera shots one by one, and showing examples in novels in which the writer has effectively used a particular camera angle (or multiple angles) to create a supercharged scene.

Varieties of Camera Angles for Specific Effects

Screenplays are structured through the use of camera direction, which becomes all-important to telling the story. The choice of camera angles within a scene affects the mood, focus, and emphasis of the story being told, and directs the viewer to pay attention to particular elements unfolding. The right camera angle will give the best impact: you wouldn't film a huge explosion using a Close-up but rather a Long Shot encompassing the wide scope of action. Writers, too, should think about not just the character POV (point of view) of a scene but the camera angles. Don't leave it up to the reader to figure out what is important to notice. Put on your director's hat and think what shots will focus on what's important. By using these filming techniques to point your reader's attention where you want it to go, you will get the results you want.

Don't Be Boring

Most authors use the same angle in every scene, and that can be boring. What do I mean by "the same angle"? I mean that if there was a camera filming what was taking place in the scene, it would be set up in one spot and never move. It would never zoom in, PAN, pull back, or follow anyone. Is that bad? Not necessarily. You may have a scene that is solely in a character's head—just her thinking. And maybe that's a powerful scene because of the character and plot points revealed. But would you enjoy reading a book in which most of the scenes were like that? Probably not. In fact, if you read a few pages of explanation and internal thinking and nothing was happening (read: no real-time playing out of a scene you can visualize), you just might throw the book down and go get a bowl of ice cream to soothe your battered soul.

It's Just Not Happening

Haven't you read scenes where two people are sitting somewhere (and you've probably not been told where) and just talking? The dialog goes on for pages, and maybe some of it is interesting, but you can't picture where these people are, what the setting is like, what they look like. Or maybe you have more description than you want—of the restaurant and their clothes and hair and the noise and smells inside. But still—nothing happens.

I'm not talking about physical action. And this is an important distinction. There can be a lot happening in a scene without a character even twitching. There can be heavy subtext, innuendo, clues, suspicions—all kinds of tension and plot reveals going on. But still, the scene can feel flat and a bit boring because it feels like the camera filming all this is stuck in one spot across the room.

This is not to say every scene needs to have your "camera" zooming and panning and doing gymnastics to keep your reader's interest up. But once you see how you can bring in a variety of camera shots to your scenes—even the ones in which not much is happening—you will realize there are better ways to construct them to supercharge them.

Don't settle for okay or boring or so-so. Think big impact. That's what great directors do. And big impact doesn't apply to just explosive scenes with high action. You can have a huge-impact small moment. A tiny element in your story can be key—the gripping pivot upon which your entire plot hinges—and by using the right camera shots, you can play up that subtle bit and blow it up to the size it should be. High-impact moments, regardless of how subtle, should "fill the entire screen." And I'll show you how it can be done.

The Art of Film Editing

Have you ever watched old black-and-white movies? I'm thinking in particular of those great Fred Astaire musicals full of amazing dance routines. Sometime, go watch a few and pay attention to the camera shot. Back in the day, film editing was kept to a minimum. It was expensive, tedious work. Film editors had to literally cut and splice pieces of film together, which was tricky to do seamlessly. Because of this, most of those great dance numbers are one long shot from one camera, without interruptions, without slicing and dicing. Not like what's done today. It makes me wonder how many takes Fred and Ginger had to do to get one good keeper shot. I get tired just thinking about all those fast, nifty steps.

Today editing is a highly praised art form, and with the current tech is much easier and versatile. A film editor must creatively work with the layers of images, story, dialogue, music, pacing, as well as the actors' performances to effectively "re-imagine" and even rewrite the film to craft a cohesive whole. Editors usually play a dynamic role in the making of a film. Walter Murch once said, "Film editing is now something almost everyone can do at a simple level and enjoy it, but to take it to a higher level requires the same dedication and persistence that any art form does."

The editing in film often goes unnoticed. However, if one does not notice the editing, then it is doing its job. The editor works on the subconscious of the viewer, and if you think about it, writers do the same when they write a novel. Editors are awarded Academy Awards, and maybe you've wondered why, but I don't.

Now, you may think it really odd, but knowing my background, you should understand when I say one of the things I pay the most attention to when I watch a movie (and comment on to my husband—to which he can attest!) is the editing. I feel the editing is what makes the movie. A terrifically edited movie scores more points in my book than a well-written one. I am enthralled when I watch a beautifully edited movie, when all the cuts of the various camera shots are pieced together like a symphony.

One movie that comes to mind is *Inception*. There are sequences in that movie that are edited to show reality unfolding on three different dream levels all at the same time. It is masterfully done. If you've watched the opening scene of *Saving Private Ryan* and you felt like your heart was being ripped out, much of that was due to the brilliant, powerful editing. Although I could barely view the painful images on the screen (and I'm glad I saw it on my small TV and not in a theater), I can't forget specific camera angles used, such as the shot taken from the seaward side of the landing craft looking toward the beach as the Allied soldiers try to disembark and are mowed down with machine-gun fire, many while still in the boat, the water turning red as bodies keep falling.

In contrast, a movie with boring editing will tend to show boring scenes that feel flat or choppy or lacking spark.

Yes, Another Hat

If you haven't figured out by now where I'm going with this, I hope you won't be surprised to have me tell you that, yes, you also need to wear that editor's hat. I don't mean the "book" kind of editor, like me, but the movie kind I mentioned above—the person who takes the film of all the raw footage of the shot scenes and pieces it together in not just the right order but in a specific sequence.

Think about it. Each scene in a movie or TV show is not just shot from one angle; it's shot from many. There are close shots in which you see one character's face and the back of another's head. There are stationary shots taken from different angles, as well as numerous moving shots taken from different angles. You may have an aerial shot, some long shots, some tilted ones, some tracking shots done with the camera moving along on a dolly. The director will make clear which shots he wants. He then, along with various producers and others, will work with the film editor to choose which shots to use in a scene, and like a jigsaw puzzle will (hopefully) seamlessly put it together so it flows without lagging, as well as provides just the right tension and pacing needed.

It's not easy. And novelists have to do exactly the same thing. They have to not only "shoot" their scenes, they have to choose the camera angles, and then piece it all together in a way that fits their genre and story, and keeps the pacing going at the speed needed to engage the reader. A novel set in Victorian England showing the characters having tea and discussing suitable marriage prospects (not my cup of tea) should have different camera shots and entirely different editing than a suspense thriller in which the protagonist has to save the world before the ticking bomb explodes.

CUT TO: An Important Point

I want to say "cut" here to emphasize something I need to talk about and will reiterate throughout this book, and that's the importance of being aware of the "high moment" of each of your scenes. This is what good directors know. Before they shoot that scene on their shooting schedule for the day, they are thinking about that instant (whether it will last a few seconds or even a minute) the scene is building to.

Without going into a treatise about scene construction (which I do in my book *Writing the Heart of Your Story*), suffice it to say each scene must have a point to it or it shouldn't be in your novel. If you have scenes with no "point," you need to either give them a point or throw them out. Too many writers write too many scenes with no point to them. Filmmaker Gustav Mercado says to create powerful impact, the technical elements, compositional choices, and narrative content should all work in context to create meaning. Without meaning, what is the point of telling your story?

Ever seen a movie that left you scratching your head? A movie with scenes that had no point to them, and for the life of you, you couldn't figure out why they were in the movie at all? Same thing. Someone should have cut those scenes out or rewritten them, you think. Maybe you've said that about scenes you've read in some novels too. Hopefully no one has said that about your novels, but if they have, you can fix that. How? By making sure you have a high moment you are building to.

A high moment doesn't have to be a huge moment. Remember, what's significant to a reader is what impacts the character. Just a single word can pack a punch in a scene, and often does. A beautifully delivered line of dialog can be more explosive than blowing up the Statue of Liberty. Great movie directors know this too. As actress Rosalind Russell said, what makes a great movie is "moments." And in order to write supercharged scenes that utilize specific camera shots, you have to know what moment you are building to. Just keep that in mind.

A String of Shots Equals a Scene

Movies are made up of a string of shot sequences—don't confuse these with whole scenes. In creating a shot sequence, the aim of using a camera is to imitate the way the human mind uses the eyes. Our minds will not let our eyes stay fixed on any one subject for more than four or five seconds. Our eyes are constantly moving and focusing on different subjects.

For example, you may be walking down the street and you come across two of your friends having a small picnic at one of the tables in the city park at the corner. Your mind will probably direct your eyes into the following views of the couple:

* First, you would have a Wide-Angle or Long Shot of the entire scene.

* As you walk toward the couple, you will look at one person, and then the other.

* As you come closer, you might shift your focus and look at what is on the table.

* Your next glance will probably be at the first person who speaks to you.

* As the conversation continues, your eyes will shift from person to person, from person to table, from an action of one person to that person's face etc., etc. The combinations could be endless.

This type of realistic behavior is what you want to capture in your fiction writing, and the way to do it is by utilizing various camera angles, the difference being that you have a specific intention in doing so. Rather than show a random encounter with boring dialog and nothing all that interesting happening in the scene—which is what real life often is like—you have an objective in playing this scene out, that high point you are leading to, a moment of revelation or plot twist that is going to deliver with a punch when you reach it. And so every camera angle is used deliberately to give the most punch when needed.

Television producers follow a basic rule that no shot should last more than thirty seconds, and no scene should last longer than three minutes. This is the 30-3 Rule. This is the basic idea of how shot sequences are made. You take one long scene and break it down into a variety of short shots.

How does this translate to fiction? A scene can take much longer than three minutes to read, and sometimes it may cover a number of moments in time, some even separated by days and weeks. But if you break down your scenes and look at the segments that take place, you will find a natural rhythm that feels just right. Scenes should be mini novels, with a beginning, middle, and end. It doesn't work to place strict rules on scenes, for they should be as long as they need to be—whatever it takes to effectively reveal the bit of storyline intended while keeping the pacing and tension taut. However, I believe if you lay out your scenes intentionally with a series of camera shots, leaving out excessive narration and backstory, your scenes will "move" like a movie and will feel like concise, succinct movie scenes.

Two Types of Camera Shots

Essentially, there are two types of camera shots—stationary and moving. I've never seen them classified this way, so I use these terms I came up with. Or you could think of them as static and dynamic, or still and kinetic. Use whatever terms work for you. But basically we're talking about filming a moment in which the camera is either moving or not moving. Simple.

You decide which types of camera shots you will use based on your high moment. If the high point of your scene involves showing an expression on someone's face, an object (like a ring), a small detail not before noticed, then the key camera shot will be a Close-up (CU), which might also be called a Close Shot, or it might be Angle On. If the high moment will be a sudden massive explosion due to an unnoticed gas leak, the key moment will require a Pull Back (PB) and/or a Long Shot (LS). By knowing the key moment and how your plot builds to it, you can plan the camera angles to best enhance the visual experience and evoke the strongest emotional reaction from your reader.

Of course, your scenes have more to them than just the high moment, and for that reason, you will need to use a number of camera angles for each scene, for the most part. But I bring up the need to first identify your high moment and determine what shot is needed then, for that's the moment of greatest impact and needs the most emphasis. Once you know how you will show that moment, you can work backward and forward, figuring out the rest of the shots. This is just my method. I have no idea if movie directors think this way or plan each scene out in any particular fashion. Maybe some work chronologically, deciding on the first shot and going from there. But I believe if you use this method, it will best serve you and the needs of your plot.

So as we go through these stationary and moving camera shots, think about when you might want to keep the "camera still" and when you want to move it from one place to another. As you will see, there's a specific purpose to each shot.

Want to read more?

You can buy *Shoot Your Novel* in paperback or as an ebook on all online venues.

Don't miss the upcoming release in The Writer's Toolbox Series:

***5 Editors Tackle the 12 Fatal Flaws of Fiction Writing*— available fall 2015!**

42443841R00146

Made in the USA
Middletown, DE
12 April 2017